MP-3 FYI

Digital Music Online

Your Q&A Guide to MP3

By Jay Lickfett

MP3 FYI

Copyright ©2000 Muska & Lipman Publishing

All rights reserved. No part of this book may be reproduced by any means without written permission from the publisher, except for brief passages for review purposes. Address all permission requests to the publisher.

All copyrights and trademarks used as examples or references in this book are retained by their individual owners.

Technology and the Internet are constantly changing, and by necessity of the lapse of time between the writing and distribution of this book, some aspects might be out of date. Accordingly, the author and publisher assume no responsibility for actions taken by readers based upon the contents of this book.

Library of Congress Number 00-100912

ISBN: 1-929685-05-X

5 4 3 2 1

Educational facilities, companies, and organizations interested in multiple copies or licensing of this book should contact the publisher for quantity discount information. Training manuals, CD-ROMs, and portions of this book are also available individually or can be tailored for specific needs.

MUSKA & LIPMAN

2645 Erie Avenue, Suite 41
Cincinnati, Ohio 45208
www.muskalipman.com
publisher@muskalipman.com

This book is composed in Glasgow, Courier and Helvetica typefaces using QuarkXpress 4.1, Adobe Photoshop 5.0.2, and Adobe Illustrator 8.0.

Created in Cincinnati, Ohio, in the United States of America.

Credits

Publisher
Andy Shafran

Managing Editor
Hope Stephan

Development Editor
Jim Chalex

Copy Editor
Kelli M. Brooks

Technical Editor
William Bruns

Proofreader
Martin Sterpka

Cover Designer
Dave Abney
John Windhorst

Production Manager
Cathie Tibbetts

Production Team
DOV Graphics
   Michelle Frey
   Stephanie Japs

Indexer
Kevin Broccoli

Printer
R.R. Donnelley and Sons

About the Author

Jay Lickfett was an early and enthusiastic adopter of MP3 and has been following the topic for several years. He teaches an online course on the subject for SmartPlanet and has covered MP3 as a columnist for the online music industry newsletter, *MusicDish*. Jay is a new technology analyst for Procter & Gamble. In his spare time, he enjoys reading, building woodworking projects, and gardening with his wife, Kara.

Acknowledgements

This book would not have been possible without the help of many others—especially the wonderful Muska & Lipman staff. I'm indebted to Andy Shafran, publisher, for his enthusiasm on the subject of MP3 and for helping at each step of the process. I'd also like to thank Hope Stephan for guiding me through the editorial process, as well as Jim Chalex, Kelli Brooks, Bill Bruns, Al Valvano, Shauna Pope, and all the others who have worked very hard to make this a better book.

Also, a very loving thank you to Kara, whose support has made all of this possible.

Table of Contents

Introduction 1

Section 1—What is MP3? 5

1—MP3—The Format

1. What is MP3? 8
2. What does MP3 stand for? 10
3. Who are these MPEG people anyway, and who listens to what they have to say? 10
4. What does Audio Layer III refer to? 12
5. Is MPEG-3 the same as MP3? 13
6. Aren't there lots of digital audio formats? Why is MP3 so popular? 14
7. Sound is either there or it isn't, right? How do you compress sound? 16
8. How does MP3 compression work? 20
9. How does MP3 encoding work? 22
10. How does MP3 decoding work? 23
11. How are compression and sound quality related for MP3 files? 23
12. If MP3 compression actually changes the sound from the original, how can you determine quality of the sound? 24
13. Does an MP3 sound as good as a CD? Can some people tell the difference? 25
14. It sounds like MPEG has the area of audio compression all locked up. How do new advances get made in this area? 26

2—MP3—the Movement

15. When and where did the MP3 movement really start to take off? 28
16. How has the recording industry reacted to MP3? 30
17. How has the MP3 movement affected artists? 33
18. How have record stores been affected by the MP3 movement? . 35
19. How do consumers benefit from MP3? 36

http://www.muskalipman.com

3—MP3 and the Law
  20 Am I going to get in trouble for this? Aren't MP3s illegal? 37
  21 Can I put MP3 files on my Web page? 41
  22 What is "fair use?". 42
  23 Can I legally copy my MP3 music onto more than one
       computer or device? 43
  24 Can I legally convert my music CDs to MP3 format? 44
  25 What laws pertain to streaming MP3s for a Net radio station? .. 44
  26 Why pay for music when I can just
       download the MP3 for free? 46

Section 2—Finding MP3 Music on the Web....... 47

4—Getting Access to MP3s
  27 What methods help me navigate to MP3s on the Internet? 50
  28 What types of MP3-related sites are there?................... 51
  29 Don't I need a really fast connection
       to the Web to get MP3 files? 55
  30 What are performance tips for regular home modem users? 57
  31 How can I schedule my MP3 downloads? 60

5—Using MP3 Portals, List Sites, and Search Engines
  32 What are some good MP3 portals and communities? 63
  33 What are some examples of MP3 list sites? 75
  34 What are some MP3 search engine sites? 77
  35 Can you help me find specific music I want? 79
  36 I get a lot of results when I search,
       but none of the links are good. How come? 80
  37 Is there a way to search multiple MP3 sites all at once,
       so I don't have to enter the same query into each one? 81
  38 How can I find artists and music I like so I don't spend
       a lot of time downloading music I think is terrible? 82
  39 What is Napster?.. 83

6—Buying MP3 Tracks
  40 Where can I buy MP3 tracks online?........................ 85
  41 What are the advantages of buying music in MP3 format? 88
  42 What are the disadvantages of buying music in MP3 format? ... 89

http://www.muskalipman.com

- 43 How do I buy an MP3 track? 90
- 44 If I buy MP3s online, how do I prove I actually paid for them? 96
- 45 What happens if my computer crashes and I lose my music? .. 97

Section 3–Listening to MP3 Music............... 99

7—Setting Up to Listen

- 46 What do I need to listen to MP3 files on my computer? 101
- 47 What are some of the best software MP3 players? 104
- 48 What are the best players for Windows? 106
- 49 What are the best players for Mac? 111
- 50 How do I play an MP3 file? 112
- 51 How do I control the volume? 115
- 52 How do I create music playlists? 116
- 53 How can I use skins? 117
- 54 How can I use plug-ins? 118

8—Net Radio—Streaming MP3

- 55 What are Net radio stations and streaming audio? 121
- 56 Why is Net radio so popular? 122
- 57 What are the major streaming audio formats? 123
- 58 What are the disadvantages of streaming audio versus downloading audio? 124
- 59 Where can I find Net radio stations? 126

9—MP3 on the Go—Portable Players

- 60 Is there a convenient way to listen to MP3 when I'm on the go? 131
- 61 I already have a portable CD player, so why would I want a portable MP3 player, too? 132
- 62 How do I get music from my computer to my portable player? 133
- 63 How do portable MP3 players store the music? 134
- 64 Can I listen to MP3 in my car? 136
- 65 What are some of the best portable MP3 players? 138

Section 4—Creating Your Own MP3 Files 141

10—Getting Ready to Rip

66 What do I need to convert my music CDs to MP3 format? 144

67 What are some of the best programs for ripping
and encoding CDs? 146

68 How can I tell if my CD-ROM drive supports
digital audio extraction? 150

69 Can I convert audio from other sources
(like LP or tape) to MP3? 151

11—Ripping and Encoding

70 What's this software going to do? 155

71 Should I use digital or analog
as the CD-ROM access method? 159

72 Should I rip to a WAV file before
encoding a track as an MP3 file? 161

73 What bitrate and encoding method should I use
when creating my MP3 files? 162

74 What is normalization? 164

75 How can I set the track information that gets displayed
by my MP3 player? 165

76 It's annoying to have to type in the
descriptive information for each MP3 track I make.
Is there a way to get it automatically? 166

12—How to Get the Most Out of Your MP3 Collection

77 Can I create regular music CDs from my MP3 collection? 167

78 What features should I consider when buying a CD-R drive? ... 168

79 What's the process for creating my own music CD? 171

80 What are music servers and how can I set up my own? 176

81 Can I create my own Net radio station to stream MP3s? 179

13—Distributing Your Own Music Using MP3

82 How can I use MP3 to get my own music out to the world? .. 183

83 How can I set up a free personal or band homepage? 184

84 How can I set up a more
customized Web site for my band? 186

85 How can I take advantage of Net radio to promote myself? ... 186

86 What are some good resources for musicians
who are interested in digital audio distribution? 187
87 How can I get my music noticed
by the industry using MP3? 187
88 Can I distribute a cover of someone else's song as an MP3? .. 188

Section 5—MP3 and the Future of Digital Audio .. 189
14—Where We Are Headed
89 What trends will influence the future of digital audio? 191
90 What is SDMI and what has been accomplished? 197
91 What other digital audio formats are out there? 199
92 Is MPEG working on any new standards? 202
93 If I make an investment in MP3 now, what happens when
the next hot format comes out? 205

Glossary 209
Index 221

Introduction

Do you enjoy listening to music—or maybe even creating your own? If so, you'll definitely want to learn more about MP3, the driving force behind a revolution in the way we find, obtain, and listen to music.

MP3 is a format for digital audio that can be played using a personal computer, special stereo components, or tiny portable players. Music in the MP3 format can be compressed to take up one-tenth of the space it uses on a normal audio compact disc, while retaining practically the same quality of the CD. The small size of MP3 audio files is very important, because it allows music to be distributed easily using the Internet. Millions of MP3 music tracks are now downloaded each day by people around the world.

The MP3 format is stirring up the music industry, giving artists and independent labels greater opportunities and consumers more choices in the way they purchase, store, and play music. While the major record companies have been unable to control illegal distribution of MP3 copies of their music online, in part because of their slowness to recognize consumers' desires to be able to download music, independent labels and artists have been quick to take advantage of MP3 for legitimate promotion and distribution of their music. This has allowed them to more effectively compete with the major labels, while consumers have enthusiastically supported MP3 for its convenience, lower cost, and the ability to find music that would otherwise be unavailable.

If MP3 sounds like something you want to know more about, *MP3 FYI* is the right book for you. In this book, we cover the most frequently asked questions about MP3, including questions about the history and technology of MP3; important digital audio legal issues; ways to find and buy MP3 on the Web; listening to MP3; and even creating your own MP3 files.

MP3 FYI is great for beginners, but it will also be very handy if you've already had some experience with MP3 and just want to make sure you're getting the most out of it.

The organization of the book is in the form of questions and answers. As well as directly answering each question, I've also tried to talk around the subject, some of the thinking behind the decisions that have been made, and other issues you might want to examine when considering the question.

The book is split into five distinct sections:

- **What is MP3?**—The first section is an introduction to the technology and history of MP3 and how the format continues to affect the music industry and the way we think about music. The legal issues of MP3 are also covered.

- **Finding MP3 Music on the Web**—In this section, you'll learn the best ways to find free MP3s, as well as how and where you can buy them.

- **Listening to MP3 Music**—The third section covers how you can listen to MP3s, both on your computer and by using portable MP3 players. Net radio stations are also covered.

- **Creating Your Own MP3 Files**—In this section, you'll learn how to create your own MP3s and how to take advantage of your growing MP3 collection. A chapter on ways you can use MP3 to promote and distribute your own music is also included here.

- **MP3 and the Future of Digital Audio**—The final section of the book covers trends in digital audio, including thoughts on the future of MP3 and competing formats.

Feel free to skip around the different sections of the book to find the answer to the particular questions you have. We'll provide you with lots of Web links to more information and resources for you to explore the world of MP3 even further.

Let's get started!

Conventions used in this book

The following conventions are used in this book:

All Web page URLs appear in **boldface**, as in **www.mp3.com**.

New terms are introduced in *italic* type, and you'll find definitions of all these terms in the Glossary, as well as a complete index, at the end of *MP3 FYI*.

Besides these terminological and typographic conventions, the book also features the following special displays for different types of important text:

> **TIP**
> Text formatted like this offers a helpful tip relevant to the topic being discussed in the main text.

> **NOTE**
> Text formatted like this highlights other interesting or useful information that relates to the topic under discussion in the main text.

Section 1
What is MP3?

1
MP3—The Format

MP3 is a format for digital audio that is sweeping the Web and the music world. It's convenient, it's fun, it's easy to share—which, we'll see, is both an advantage and a disadvantage at times.

MP3 is more than a music format—it's a phenomenon. MP3 provides new and better ways of doing things for artists *and* music listeners. For example, artists can choose to take their music directly to retailers and listeners, without having to deal with a traditional record company. Consumers get lower prices, more convenient ways to obtain music, and access to many artists they might otherwise never hear, just to name a few of the many benefits of MP3.

MP3 has been a hot topic in the news lately, so you might already be familiar with it. Even if you've had some experience with MP3, you'll still enjoy this chapter. We'll start with where MP3 came from and the ideas behind how it works.

MP3—The Format

Q1. What is MP3?

MP3 is a format for storing and transmitting sound. MP3-formatted sound is usually dealt with as a file that can be saved on a computer disk or stored in the memory of a portable MP3 player. These MP3 files are much like document and spreadsheet files in that you need additional software to actually use them. In the case of MP3 files, you need software in order to either listen to the music on your computer or to download it to a portable MP3 player that you can take with you wherever you go.

MP3-formatted music doesn't always have to be a file saved on your computer or some other device. In fact, you can listen to Net radio stations playing MP3 music without needing to permanently store an MP3 file on your computer. We'll cover Net radio and the process used to get the MP3 music to you in **Chapter 8**, "Net Radio—Streaming MP3." The MP3 format has two key features that make it very exciting:

- MP3 compresses the audio, so it takes up much less disk space.

    The big deal about MP3 is that it lets you store music in a way that takes up much less disk space than other typical formats, such as *WAV* files. In fact, MP3 can squeeze audio into less than one-tenth the space it normally takes up on a CD.

    #### You'll be happy to wave goodbye to WAV

    WAV is a very common file format for storing audio on PCs. WAV files almost always use a method of representing the audio called "pulse code modulation" *(PCM)*, which is the way audio is stored on music CDs.

Because PCM does not compress the audio, a music CD can hold only about 74 minutes of audio and WAV files can take up a lot of space on a computer disk. A WAV file recorded at CD quality using PCM would take up about 40 MB of space for a typical four-minute track. That same track stored as an MP3 would require about 4 MB of space.

The fact that the file takes up less space on your computer's disk is great news, but the best part of making a file smaller is that it takes less time to move it across a network like the Internet. Due to the large amount of information it takes to represent music digitally, and the correspondingly large size of audio files, in the past it was impractical to download high-quality music over anything but a very fast network connection. MP3 greatly improves the speed of downloads and makes it much more tolerable for people with slower connections, such as typical 56k modems.

▶ The quality of the audio remains very high after *compression*.

The second important aspect of MP3 is that even though it's compressed to take up less space, the quality of the audio is very good. Although MP3 isn't perfect, it's quite difficult to hear the difference between a song played directly from a CD and one compressed to MP3 format, making MP3 ideal for all but the most demanding of audio applications. You might compare the quality difference between MP3 and CD audio to the case of a reproduction lithograph of an original art print. The original print may be of slightly better quality, but many people would find the reproduction perfectly acceptable, especially considering the price difference. Similarly, most people find that the convenience of MP3 greatly outweighs the nearly imperceptible quality difference between it and CD audio.

Q2 What does MP3 stand for?

MP3 is the file extension and name commonly used to refer to the Motion Picture Experts Group *(MPEG)*, Audio Layer III file format. Don't you agree that MP3 is much easier to say than that mouthful? Read on to the next couple of questions to learn more about who the Motion Picture Experts are and what Layer III refers to.

Q3 Who are these MPEG people anyway, and who listens to what they have to say?

MPEG (which stands for Motion Picture Experts Group) is a group of people who work to define international standards for storing and transmitting video and audio. They are a part of the much broader *International Organization for Standardization (ISO)*, a group composed of representatives from standards organizations from more than 125 countries. The ISO deals with standards for all imaginable types of technology.

To learn more about the ISO and the various areas it's working in, check out the organization's Web site at **www.iso.ch**. The official Web site of MPEG is **drogo.cselt.it/mpeg/**.

International Standards—Who Cares?

International standards are carefully defined and documented technical agreements that precisely describe a specific material, finished product, or a process. Standards are definitely a good thing, both for businesses and for those of us who buy the products made by those businesses.

Standards help businesses compete in the global market by improving the quality and reliability of material and products, as well as guaranteeing their interoperability with similar products from competitors. For those of us using the finished product, this means we can count on it working in the way we expect. The competition between the producers of compatible products also results in lower prices and better products.

We take advantage of standards every day without even thinking about it. For example, ISO defined the speed ratings for photographic film for your camera and even the physical dimensions for credit cards. So the next time the clerk swipes your card at the store to pay for your purchase, thank ISO for helping define the global standard.

MPEG releases standards in phases, which it designates with Arabic numerals, such as MPEG-1, MPEG-2, and so on. The *MPEG-1* standard was published in 1993, and the second phase, *MPEG-2*, was published in 1995. Work on an MPEG-3 standard (which is unrelated to MP3—see **Question 5**) was started but canceled, while two new standards, designated *MPEG-4* and *MPEG-7*, are currently in the works. The audio portion of the MPEG-2 standard is backward-compatible with MPEG-1 Audio. However, the MPEG-4 and MPEG-7 standards are much different and are not backward-compatible with other standards. We'll talk more about MPEG-4 and MPEG-7 in **Chapter 14**, "Where We Are Headed." The audio portion of the MPEG standards can be used separately from the video or combined audio and video portions. So in our exploration of MP3, we'll stick to the audio aspect of the MPEG standards.

MPEG Audio has been adopted for use in many applications, including broadcasting, storage and editing of audio, computer multimedia, and telecommunications. Some uses of MPEG Audio include the following:

▶ Digital radio broadcasting (ADR, DAB, Digital Radio [US], Worldspace Radio)
▶ Cable/satellite TV (USSB, DirecTV, etc.)
▶ Internet radio
▶ Home recording studios

http://www.muskalipman.com

- Storage in various formats (CD-i, CD-Video, DVD)
- Computer-based multimedia
- Audio/Videoconferencing over ISDN lines

Some of these applications actually use MPEG Audio Layer III (MP3), while others use either Layer I or Layer II, which are additional audio formats defined as a part of the MPEG-1 and MPEG-2 standards. We'll talk more about these three layers in the next question.

> **TIP**
> If you want to learn more about the MPEG organization or its standards, check out the official MPEG Web page at **drogo.cselt.it/mpeg/**.

Q4 What does Audio Layer III refer to?

Both MPEG-1 Audio and MPEG-2 Audio include a family of three closely related methods of compressing audio. These methods are known as Layer I, Layer II, and *Layer III*. The Audio Layer III in MP3 refers to the use of the most advanced of these compression methods, Layer III.

Each of the three layers has its advantages in different situations, and that's why the MPEG Audio standards define three methods rather than just one. Of the three methods, Layer I compresses audio the least, but it requires the simplest software for creating and listening to the audio. Layer II is able to compress the audio to a greater degree, but it also requires more complex software, particularly in the creation of the compressed file. Because the software is more complex, this also means that the compression process is slower and requires a more powerful computer. Layer III is the best of the three methods as far as compression is concerned, and as a result requires the most complex software.

Layer III has become the most popular of the three for digital music because of its greater compression, which made it much more practical for downloading and storing. This led to most software for *creating* digital audio being focused on Layer III, though most MP3 playing software can also play Layer I and Layer II files.

The Layer III compression scheme was developed in large part by researchers at the *Fraunhofer Institute for Integrated Circuits* in Germany and was selected by the MPEG organization to be incorporated into its standards.

> **NOTE**
> If you're interested in more technical details of the Layer III method of compression developed at the Fraunhofer Institute, this Web page may be of interest:
> **www.iis.fhg.de/amm/techinf/layer3/index.html.**

Q5 Is MPEG-3 the same as MP3?

Although it sounds similar, MPEG-3 isn't the same as MP3. If it had been completed, MPEG-3 would have been the next standard in the series following MPEG-1 and MPEG-2. MPEG-3 was intended to be used to define a transmission format for high definition TV (HDTV), but it was discovered that the MPEG-2 standard could be used for that purpose, making a new MPEG-3 standard unnecessary.

http://www.muskalipman.com

Aren't there lots of digital audio formats? Why is MP3 so popular?

MP3 has some obvious advantages over uncompressed audio formats, which can get smaller file sizes only by severely degrading the sound. However, there are a number of competing audio formats besides MP3 that also use compression, some of which are actually better in compressing audio files. Why has MP3 remained so popular in spite of the availability of technically superior alternative formats?

The main reason is probably the simple fact that MP3 was the first popular way for the typical home computer user to download and store high-quality music files. Sometimes just being first can make a huge difference!

This wide acceptance of MP3, beginning in 1997, was a result of several factors, including the availability (and affordability) of more powerful personal computers, increased use of the Internet, and availability of software to play MP3 tracks.

The software needed to listen to MP3 files is more complex than the software used for uncompressed WAV files and the like, because an MP3 player must first decompress the file in a step called *decoding* (see **Figure 1.1**). This decoding step requires quite a bit of work on the part of the computer's processor and, practically speaking, this means a Pentium-class or Power Mac computer is needed to listen to MP3 files. As these computers have gotten cheaper and started to show up in households, more and more people have been able to take advantage of the MP3 format.

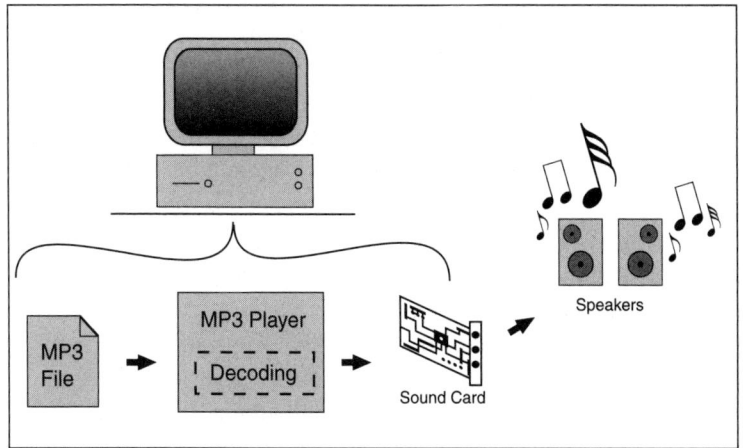

Figure 1.1 An MP3 file must be decoded in order to be played.

> **TIP**
>
> The portable MP3 playing devices that are becoming popular use specialized processors and software to play the MP3 files that are downloaded to them. By optimizing them to do just one thing—play MP3 audio—these seemingly simple devices accomplish the same thing it takes a Pentium or better general purpose personal computer to do. We'll take a look at a number of these devices in Chapter 9, "MP3 on the Go—Portable Players."

Sound is either there or it isn't, right? How do you compress sound?

In order to understand how audio compression works, you first have to have an understanding of what sound is and the difference between representing sound by *analog* or *digital* means. Sound is a vibration of molecules surrounding a vibrating object, such as a piano string. These vibrations can be passed though a medium like air or water as a wave, with the molecules of the medium alternately being compressed and returning to their original position as the sound wave passes through. If a sound wave is converted from a mechanical vibration to an electrical representation of the same wave using a microphone, it is known as an analog signal (see **Figure 1.2**). In an analog signal, varying electrical voltages represent the analogous varying pressures of the sound wave, and these electrical voltages may be stored in order to recreate the original sound.

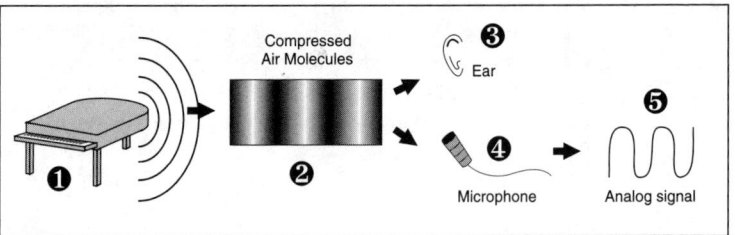

Figure 1.2 A sound wave is converted to an analog electrical signal.

❶ Vibration of piano strings cause ❷ a sound wave which travels through the air, ❸ is heard by listeners, ❹ and is picked up by a microphone. ❺ The microphone transforms the sound wave into an analog signal—an electronic representation.

To be stored on a computer, an analog signal must be converted to a digital one. This is accomplished in a process called *sampling*, in which the analog voltage signal is measured repeatedly at a very rapid rate. The sampling process is performed by an analog-to-digital converter (ADC), which provides a binary value of the voltage at each sample point that can be stored and processed by digital electronic equipment (see **Figure 1.3**). This digital output can be considered to be uncompressed digital audio.

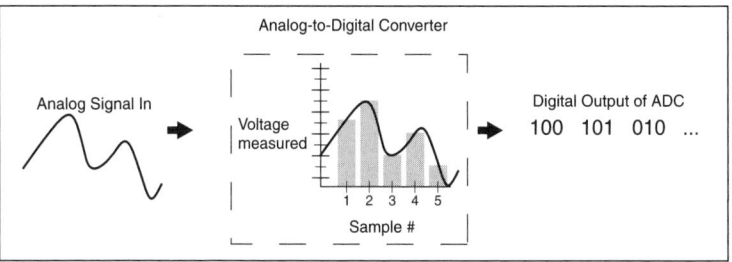

Figure 1.3 An analog-to-digital converter transforms an analog signal into a digital representation.

Several factors affect the quality of the sampled digital audio, and these can also be manipulated to reduce the amount of space needed to represent the audio signal. The factors are as follows:

- Frequency of sampling
- Resolution of sampling
- Number of channels sampled

One way of reducing the space needed to store audio is to reduce the frequency of sampling, or the number of times per second the voltage of the analog signal is measured. Although this results in less data to store, it also means the audio quality is reduced. This is because of a rule in acoustics called the Nyquist Theorem, which states that the sampling rate must be at least twice the frequency of the sound you want to reproduce. In other words, if you don't sample fast enough you will start to lose the treble portion of your audio. Since the top frequency that can be heard by people is around 20 kHz, sampling at anything less than 40 kHz (40,000 samples per second) will likely cause noticeable quality loss in the audio. By way of example, CD-quality audio uses a sampling frequency of 44,100 samples per second, whereas telephone quality audio requires only about 8,000 samples per second.

Another way of manipulating the amount of storage needed for digital audio is to adjust the sampling resolution, which is the number of digits needed to represent the voltage value measured for each sample. The number of digits allowed (*bits* of resolution) determines the number of distinct voltage levels that can be used to describe the analog signal. Since any in-between values are rounded off in the analog-to-digital conversion, the more distinct levels there are, the more closely the digital signal will match the original analog one (see **Figure 1.4**). In fact, each additional bit of resolution adds 6 decibels to the signal-to-noise ratio, which results in less background noise.

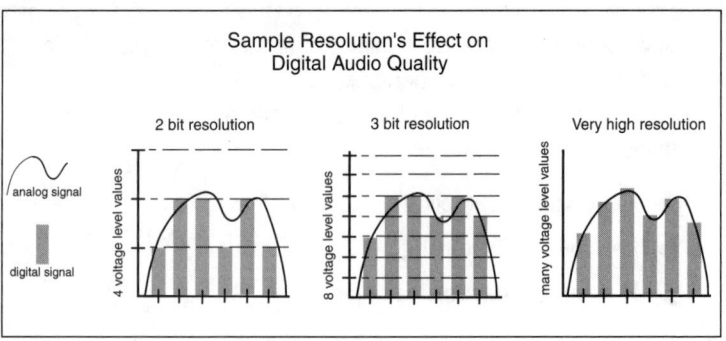

Figure 1.4 The greater the sampling resolution, the closer the digital representation of the audio will be to the original analog signal.

CD-quality audio typically requires 16-bit sampling resolution (65,536 possible levels), whereas 8-bit resolution (256 levels) is good enough for telephone-quality sound. So, reducing sample resolution reduces the space needed to store audio, but it can also result in noticeable background noise.

Reducing the number of channels recorded is another way audio can be made to fit in less storage space. One channel of audio (monophonic) requires less information than two-channel stereo sound, but, of course, it doesn't sound as good, provided the rest of the system supports a stereo signal.

Data compression is the science of coding information in a specific way to use a smaller amount of storage space than is normally used. After audio is in a digital format, it can be compressed using one of a number of techniques, just as other types of data such as text documents and pictures can be compressed. Because certain patterns are more common in different types of data, specialized methods of compression are often developed to maximize performance for each type of data. MPEG Audio Layer III is one such specialized compression algorithm for sound. Specifically, MP3 is an audio compression method designed to be used in applications that require relatively low bitrates.

Bitrate is a measure that can be used to describe the amount of compression achieved on sound. It represents the amount of data that is required to capture the audio so it can be reproduced. So, the lower the bitrate for a given clip of audio, the more you can consider it compressed. A typical bitrate for a stereo, CD-quality MP3 is 128kbps (1 kbps = 1000 bits per second), compared to the bitrate of 1400kbps for 16-bit, stereo, CD audio sampled at 44.1 kHz when represented in PCM.

http://www.muskalipman.com

Q8 How does MP3 compression work?

In the answer to the previous question, you saw that there is generally a tradeoff between sound quality and the amount of compression that can be applied to digital audio. MP3 finds a way to twist the rules by taking advantage of the way our brains process sound. By determining what portions of the audio we wouldn't hear anyway and removing them, MP3 can compress audio with little apparent impact on the quality of the sound.

The key characteristic of our auditory system that MP3 utilizes is the fact that we can't distinguish weak sounds when they occur at the same time as a louder sound of nearly the same frequency. This principle is known as auditory *masking*. A masking effect can be easily experienced using a recording that has some background noise present due to low sampling resolution. During quiet moments or breaks in the music, the noise might be very conspicuous, but when the music is loud the noise can't be heard.

MP3 uses strong sounds as an opportunity to use fewer bits to represent that portion of the frequency spectrum, even though that raises the noise level. This works because as long as the noise is masked by the strong sound, the listener does not notice much change in the audio quality. Any time fewer bits can be used to represent the audio, greater compression is achieved.

Stronger and weaker sounds occurring simultaneously aren't the only type of masking effect that can be used by MP3 compression. There are also masking effects before and after strong sounds. In other words, it takes a small amount of time for the brain to process the change in sound level around a strong sound, and this is another opportunity for MP3 to use fewer bits for that portion of the audio.

There can be many masking effects overlapping and interacting with one another in any given moment of audio, and MP3 compression takes these interactions into account. MP3 encoding also considers the fact that the range of human hearing is between 20Hz and 20kHz and that our hearing is most sensitive in the 2-4kHz range of human speech (see **Figure 1.5**).

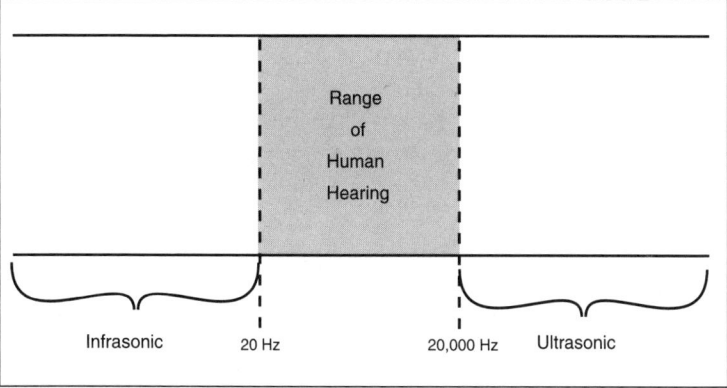

Figure 1.5 MP3 can also ignore frequencies outside the range of normal human hearing.

The science of figuring out how we perceive sound is known as psychoacoustics. So, the MP3 coding scheme is said to be utilizing a *psychoacoustic model* when it determines which parts of the audio it can leave out of an MP3 encoded file.

> **TIP**
> To learn more about psychoacoustic models and MP3, check out the "What is MPEG-Audio" section of the MPEG FAQ at **www.mpeg1.de/mpegfaq/**, or the Fraunhofer Institute's "Basics of Perceptual Audio Coding" page at **www.iis.fhg.de/amm/techinf/basics.html**.

Psychoacoustic methods aren't the only means of compression used by MP3. Additional compression is achieved by handling stereo information more efficiently than simply allocating half of the bits available to each channel. MP3 can allocate bits between the channels as needed based on the complexity of each (simple stereo mode), or it can encode one channel with the portion of the audio that is identical across both source channels while putting the difference in the second channel (joint stereo mode). Joint stereo mode tends to be most efficient and retains all of the stereo information of the original. MP3 also utilizes a type of data compression called Huffman coding, which replaces commonly repeating patterns with shorter patterns that can be translated back when the files are decoded.

Q9 How does MP3 encoding work?

The actual process of creating an MP3 file from the original audio information is called *encoding*. As the encoder analyzes the input audio using filters that represent the psychoacoustic model, it tries to meet the masking requirements (so that no noticeable differences will be heard) and the bitrate requirements. MP3 supports bitrates ranging from 8kbps to 320kbps, so as to provide the best tradeoff between compression and quality for a number of different applications. The typical bitrate used for CD-quality audio is 128kbps, but lower bitrates are also often used when greater compression is needed and lower quality is acceptable to the listener.

The encoder saves several kinds of information to make up the completed MP3 file. One part is all of the frequency data not filtered out by masking. The encoder also must save information that describes how the encoder allocated bits for the frequency information. This additional data is called side information and is used like a legend on a map by the decoder to recreate the audio when it is played back.

Because the encoding step requires all of the calculations for determining the masking threshold and the bit allocation, it turns out to be the most complex and, therefore, most time-consuming part of the encoding/decoding process.

Q10 How does MP3 decoding work?

MP3 decoding converts the compressed MP3 audio back into a form that can be sent out to the sound card and speakers in your computer. Any software that can play MP3 has a decoder built into it.

A decoder is much simpler than an encoder because it doesn't need to have the psychoacoustic model or bit allocation components that are required in the encoder. The decoder just has to be able to use the coded signal and side information to re-create the audio.

Q11 How are compression and sound quality related for MP3 files?

Even though MP3 takes advantage of the way we perceive audio to compress the audio with as little loss of quality as possible, there is still a tradeoff between compression and sound quality. However, MP3 compression results in very little loss of quality when compared to other means of making sound files smaller, such as reducing the sampling frequency or resolution.

Following are some typical guidelines given by the Fraunhofer Institute for quality versus compression:

Table 1.1—Fraunhofer Institute Guidelines for Quality versus Compression

Sound Quality	Compression Ratio	Bitrate
Better than Shortwave (mono)	48:1	16kbps
Better than AM Radio (mono)	24:1	32kbps
Similar to FM Radio (stereo)	24:1	64kbps
Similar to CD (stereo)	10:1	128kbps

If MP3 compression actually changes the sound from the original, how can you determine quality of the sound?

Because MP3 compression depends on perception, rather than the actual similarity of the encoded sound and the original, most traditional methods of measuring audio quality—including signal-to-noise ratio, total harmonic distortion, and bandwidth—do not have much meaning for MP3 tracks. The encoding process might even intentionally introduce noise or distortion as long as the perceived audio quality is maintained.

Listening tests were used during the creation of the MPEG Audio standards to measure the quality of the various techniques. In these tests, trained listeners heard and rated audio tracks carefully selected to show the limits of the technology. The test format consists of playing an audio clip three times. The listener hears the original first, then rates the two subsequent clips, one of which is encoded. Listening tests of this type provide objective results but are very expensive to conduct.

> **TIP**
> To get an idea of what some listening samples are like, check out the following: **www.tnt.uni-hannover.de/project/mpeg/audio/sqam/**.

A new quality measurement called *Noise-to-Mask Ratio*, which is based on psychoacoustic principles, has been developed by the Fraunhofer Institute and may eventually eliminate or reduce the need for expensive listening tests.

Does an MP3 sound as good as a CD? Can some people tell the difference?

MP3 audio isn't perfect by its very nature, and through careful listening it is possible to detect the slight differences between an MP3 and the original source. This means MP3 isn't a good choice for applications where the very highest sound quality is required. However, for many applications, the benefits of MP3 greatly outweigh the slight quality drop from the original.

For example, if you're playing music at a party, no one is going to be able to hear the difference between music played from a CD and music played from an MP3 file, and the convenience of being able to set up a long playlist of MP3 tracks makes it an easy choice. Or, if you want to download some tracks to a tiny portable MP3 player, you may be willing to give up some quality in order to squeeze more songs into the memory of the player. On the other hand, if you're trying to make a high-fidelity recording that you're later going to listen to very closely with no distractions, then MP3 probably isn't the right choice of formats.

 **It sounds like MPEG has the area of audio compression all locked up. How do new advances get made in this area?**

You might wonder how advances in audio compression technology get put into practice, if MPEG is generally in charge of defining standards for video and audio compression. Fortunately, this problem was considered when the MPEG Audio standards were created. There are two main ways in which new developments can be incorporated into the MPEG standards.

The first way is the standards process itself. When beginning new phases of the standards process, MPEG accepts proposals of new technology, and these proposals are evaluated against one another. In the case of MPEG Audio Layer III, it was technology from the Fraunhofer Institute that was accepted.

Acceptance as a standard doesn't take away patent protections from the developer of the technology. In the case of MP3, the Fraunhofer Institute as well as Thompson Multimedia hold key patents on the technology, and they collect royalties when it is used.

The second method in which new developments can be taken advantage of is by making the standard flexible. This is done by making the standard specify both the way the encoded information is represented and the way a decoder must work, while not specifying the exact process that should be used for encoding. This allows the encoding software to be specialized for the particular application, as long as the encoded audio can be uncompressed by a compliant decoder.

2
MP3—the Movement

There is much more to the MP3 story than just technology. MP3 is a key driver of the digital music revolution that is reshaping the way consumers obtain and listen to music, and it is broadening the options for artists seeking to market and distribute their work. This MP3 movement is being promoted by a community of music lovers and artists who have discovered new and better ways of doing things using the power of the Internet.

When combined with MP3, the Web opens up marketing and distribution of music to individuals, in addition to the traditional industry players (just as the Web has made it possible for writers to publish their work for a global audience). The Web and MP3 have lowered the cost of entry and allowed artists direct access to consumers, shifting the balance of power in the music industry toward independent artists and consumers. As the digital music revolution continues to play out, the combination of MP3 and the Web will dramatically affect consumers, artists, record companies, radio stations, and other players in the recording industry.

Q15 When and where did the MP3 movement really start to take off?

MP3 has been the format of choice in this revolution, largely because of its openness and convenience—attributes that allowed it to fit well within the culture of the Internet and the Web. The Web has always enjoyed a culture of sharing and free flow of information. E-commerce and "dot com" mania may have captured much of the media spotlight of late, but the free exchange of information and the development of sharing communities remain central themes of the Internet. These themes have allowed an extensive grassroots effort in support of the MP3 format to flourish on the Web. Other proprietary formats have not enjoyed the same success, in part because they have been more restrictive and haven't fit as well within Web culture.

The open nature of MP3 started with its definition in the open MPEG standards in the early 1990s. As a result, anyone who wants to license MP3 technology and incorporate it into a product can do so. The German Fraunhofer Institute, which played a central role in the development of MP3 technology, even posted free source code for a sample MP3 decoder, the basis for MP3-playing software. Because of the open standard and freely available seed code, MP3 software has flourished.

One example of the MP3 players that were developed in this early environment is Winamp, which today is one of the most popular and successful MP3 players in the world. Justin Frankel created Winamp in April 1997, and it originally used freely available code from another MP3 player called amp. As new versions of Winamp included more and more features, an active and vocal user community provided feedback and new ideas, aiding Winamp's success. We'll discuss how to use the Winamp player in **Chapter 7**, "Setting Up to Listen."

> **NOTE**
>
> Software developers have greatly aided the MP3 movement by often sharing their source code (the programming instructions that make up software) for playing MP3s with one another in a way that allowed continuous improvement by others with new ideas. For example, many MP3 players have been based on the code of Tomislav Uzelac's amp decoder, which he released freely for noncommercial use in the mid-1990s. This sharing of code has occasionally led to ruffled feathers—Uzelac's PlayMedia Systems sued and later settled with Nullsoft over a dispute involving alleged unlicensed use of amp code in Winamp. However, the benefits of sharing MP3 decoder source code have greatly outweighed the occasional problems.
>
> Several major MP3-related open-source projects are under way, including FreeAmp and icecast. FreeAmp (**www.freeamp.org**) is a very nice MP3 player with versions for Windows and Linux (a Mac version is expected soon). The FreeAmp project is being sponsored by EMusic.com, but the code is still freely available to anyone who wishes to download it. Icecast is open-source server software that allows Net radio broadcasting that is compatible with Nullsoft's SHOUTcast streaming MP3 server (see **Chapter 8**, "Net Radio–Streaming MP3"). The icecast project has also attracted a corporate sponsor—in this case, the online media company iCAST. These efforts show that the grassroots enthusiasm behind MP3 software continues today.

With the increasing availability of software for using MP3 and increasing awareness of the format among Web users, the MP3 movement began to acquire some momentum, particularly among those with access to fast networks, such as university students. MP3 tracks could be copied and spread quickly, and large, shared collections of pirated music became more prevalent. This availability of in-demand music continues to drive the success of the MP3 format. In late 1998, the MP3 movement got another huge boost as a result of media attention brought about by several lawsuits. These lawsuits were initiated by the music industry against Diamond Multimedia, the manufacturer of the Rio portable MP3 player.

The explosive growth of the Web has had a lot to do with its ability to present graphics and audio in a way that really excites people. The MP3 movement has been a key part of this, since it helps artists and music lovers share and find music. Music will continue to proliferate on the Web—either as MP3 or in new formats—as long as there are creative people who love to listen to and create music.

Q16 How has the recording industry reacted to MP3?

By mid-1997, the recording industry was beginning to take notice of the MP3 phenomenon, which allowed easy pirating of music. Music pirates could copy MP3 files much more easily than they could manufacture illegal CDs, and this opened up a whole new area that the industry had to confront. In June 1997, the Recording Industry Association of America *(RIAA)* filed suits against three Internet MP3 archive site operators, charging them with illegally reproducing and distributing copyrighted music. Although actions against music pirates were expected, many in the MP3 community felt that the music industry was attacking the MP3 format when the RIAA attempted to block the sale of the Rio portable MP3 player.

> **NOTE**
> The Recording Industry Association of America is a trade organization that represents music industry financial and legal interests. Among other things, it works to influence legislation, protect the intellectual property rights of artists and record companies, and fight music piracy worldwide.
>
> The homepage of the RIAA can be found at (**www.riaa.com**).

Diamond Multimedia's Rio allowed convenient playing of MP3 away from a computer and MP3 player software. Although it could be used to play illegally obtained MP3 tracks, it could also be used for legitimate MP3 tracks downloaded from the Web or created by the owner of the device. The RIAA lawsuit charged Diamond with violating the *Audio Home Recording Act (AHRA)* of 1992, which requires that digital recording devices include the serial copy management system (SCMS) to prevent unlimited digital copying of music. Diamond argued that the Rio was a computer peripheral, not a recording device, which would exempt it from the SCMS requirement. Following countersuits and appeals, a U.S. Court of Appeals finally ruled in June 1999 that the Rio did not violate the AHRA and that copyright law allows consumers to transfer music they own to portable devices for their own use. Ironically, the extensive publicity the lawsuits brought to the Rio and the MP3 movement only helped to intensify the interest in the MP3 format.

In response to the threat to the traditional music industry resulting from pirating of MP3 tracks, the industry has created the Secure Digital Music Initiative (SDMI), which is charged with devising a means of providing digital audio in a way that maintains control over distribution and licensing. It remains to be seen if the SDMI system will be as convenient and easy as MP3 so that consumers will accept it. We'll discuss SDMI further in **Chapter 14**, "Where We Are Headed." The music industry so far has been reluctant to use MP3 for legitimate distribution of music, even with the new opportunities it affords for promotional marketing and lower-cost distribution. The reluctance is due mainly to concerns about the ease of piracy and the loss of control over the distribution of the music. However, many people have argued that piracy will happen no matter what the industry does, because people will always be able to convert digital audio that is secured using schemes like SDMI into an unprotected format such as MP3.

http://www.muskalipman.com

Why do so many people in the MP3 community dislike the RIAA?

Many MP3 enthusiasts have developed a negative opinion of the RIAA because of its positions in the Rio lawsuit and its support of the SDMI effort. However, the recording industry's concern over piracy is quite legitimate—after all, billions of dollars are lost due to piracy each year, and it's primarily the record companies and artists who lose this money. Why isn't the MP3 community behind the RIAA's actions?

For the most part, it isn't the RIAA's stand against piracy that turns off the MP3 community. Many people who use MP3 are themselves musicians whose livelihoods depend on music, and many other MP3 enthusiasts are music lovers who've invested lots of money in purchasing the albums of their favorite artists. The real issue is control and, in particular, who gets to control how consumers use and listen to music that they own. Consumers want to be able to listen to their music in many different formats—on a CD, as an MP3, or however it is most convenient for them. No one wants to have to keep buying the same music over and over as the media it comes on changes. The perception of many throughout the Rio lawsuit was that the RIAA was trying to control how consumers have to listen to music they own legitimately. The SDMI effort has also added to concerns of many consumers that the recording industry's interests seem more in tune with controlling music than meeting listeners' wishes. In order for the RIAA to gain the support of the MP3 community, it will have to find a way to protect the rights of record companies and artists in a way that doesn't trample the rights of consumers.

By early 2000, several of the major labels were beginning to move cautiously toward more electronic distribution of music, though still not in MP3 format. In February, EMI announced a deal with Supertracks to create a secure system for distributing EMI's music to music retailer Musicland's online stores, such as SamGoody.com and Suncoast.com. The system built for EMI will use the *EPAC* secure digital audio format rather than MP3 (for more on EPAC, see **Question 91**). Another major label—Universal—planned to have its digital distribution system in place by mid-2000. In addition to their individual efforts, all of the big five labels (BMG Entertainment, EMI Music, Universal Music Group, Warner Music Group, and Sony Music Entertainment) have made investments in the Listen.com portal, which is a directory of legal digital music downloads on the Web (see **Chapter 5**, "Using MP3 Portals, List Sites, and Search Engines").

The recording industry is in a tough position. The major labels still have a lot to offer artists, including marketing power and money for promotion, but they will need to find a way to take advantage of those aspects of their business in an age when anyone can distribute music.

Q17 How has the MP3 movement affected artists?

The MP3 movement is profoundly changing the way artists deal with record companies and with their fans.

Quite a few well-known artists, such as the Beastie Boys, Public Enemy, and Alanis Morissette, have released promotional MP3 tracks. These tracks are often remixes or new songs released only as MP3 to satisfy agreements with the artist's record company. Most artists signed with the major record companies are being held back by the reluctance of the record company to release large numbers of tracks before SDMI gives them a secure format.

http://www.muskalipman.com

Much of the beneficial change the MP3 movement brings is for independent artists. Using MP3 and the Web, these artists can potentially reach and distribute their music to millions of people without even having to sign with a record company (see **Figure 2.1**). However, many artists choose to go with an independent label that distributes using the Web. Doing this gives them the advantage of help with promoting their music, but they still keep a much larger portion of the profit than they would with a major label because there are fewer costs associated with distribution by downloading. These independent labels can also afford to take on many artists who wouldn't get contracts with the major record companies, because they don't have to recover as much to break even due to the lower costs of promotion and distribution via the Web and MP3.

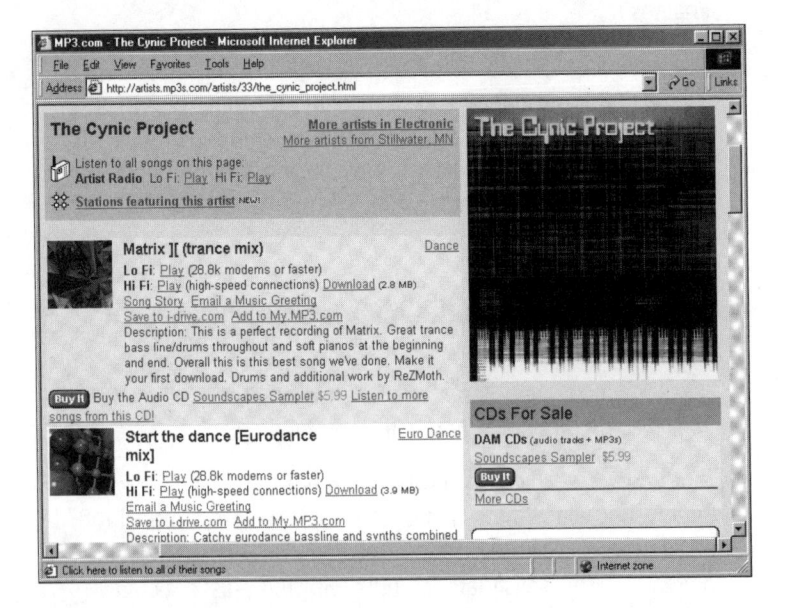

Figure 2.1 The Cynic Project is an artist using MP3.com to market his music.

There are already success stories of several independent artists who've signed contracts with major labels after marketing themselves online using MP3. One example is Fisher, a pop act that made a name for itself distributing tracks on MP3.com (**artists.mp3s.com/artists/14/fisher1.html**). Fisher signed a contract with FarmClub.com/Interscope Records in March 2000.

Q18 How have record stores been affected by the MP3 movement?

As a result of the MP3 movement, retail record stores probably stand to lose the most of any party involved. Not only does piracy affect their sales (assuming most people don't also buy the CD), but legal digital audio distribution will certainly hurt them as it becomes more and more the method of choice for people to buy music. For example, as portable car and stereo component players for MP3 and other digital audio formats become increasingly common, people will be less likely to need to buy music in CD format. Record stores that are Internet based, such as CDNOW, may be much better positioned for the transition between distribution of music on a physical medium, like a CD, to distribution of just the music itself as MP3 or other digital audio format.

Record stores in your local mall aren't going to disappear any time soon, or maybe ever, but they will certainly begin to change the services they offer. For example, Virgin Megastores in the U.S. and Canada now have kiosks that allow customers to browse a catalog of tracks including artists from Sony and EMI and purchase the tracks for download to a portable digital audio player.

Q19 How do consumers benefit from MP3?

Consumers are huge winners with MP3. MP3 makes getting music more convenient. With MP3, you can browse, sample, and download MP3 tracks from the comfort of your home computer, saving a trip to the record store. Consumers can find a huge selection of artists and albums online, including independent and new artists who don't have wide distribution (or any distribution) in record stores. Consumers also benefit from lower prices, because the cost of distribution is less than with physical inventory and because you can purchase just the tracks you like. Plus, you won't ever see "Out of Stock" on an album being sold as a downloadable MP3!

MP3 also makes it easier for consumers to manage and enjoy their music collection. A large music collection can be stored and organized on a personal computer and played through your stereo or downloaded to a portable MP3 player. MP3 makes it easy to set up long playlists without swapping tapes or CDs, and with some car MP3 players, you can have access to your entire music collection through your car stereo without ever having to change a CD.

Additionally, hundreds of MP3 Net radio stations broadcast everything from Top 40 hits to talk radio, providing consumers with access to a much greater selection than their local over-the-air radio stations can provide.

Perhaps the greatest consumer win is that the MP3 movement is forcing the music industry (which hasn't had to deal with much technological change since CDs became popular) to innovate in order to survive. The new capabilities offered by MP3 and the ongoing shakeup of the music industry translate to a more enjoyable music experience for consumers.

3
MP3 and the Law

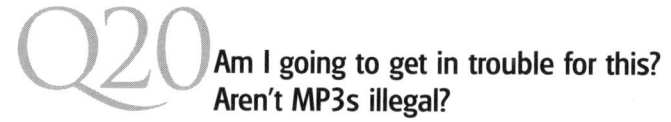

Q20. Am I going to get in trouble for this? Aren't MP3s illegal?

By itself, MP3 is neither legal nor illegal. How it's used is what's important. In this respect, MP3 is like many other tools or technologies you deal with every day. Kitchen knives aren't illegal, even though they can be used to hurt someone instead of creating a culinary masterpiece. Watching cable or satellite TV is fine, although some people might steal service or descramble channels without paying. Although there are many examples of illegal use, MP3 can be used for legitimate purposes.

There has been a stigma associated with MP3 because there *is* a lot of pirated music online in the format, and representatives of the music industry sometimes seem to attack the format rather than the problem of the piracy. This stigma is actively counteracted by those who see MP3 as great for legitimate use.

One way to approach this problem is through better education on just what is allowed and what isn't. Book publishers have used education as a followup to their lawsuit against Kinko's in the early 1990s. In that case, Kinko's was found to be distributing photocopies of copyrighted works without paying the owners. Since the lawsuit, Kinko's has posted notices describing the pertinent laws to help educate customers on when they can and can't copy material. While it certainly doesn't completely prevent illegal copying, it probably cuts down on it. A similar education campaign for MP3 might reduce piracy by helping people understand when they're breaking the law and what consequences they may face if they are caught. In fact, the RIAA is attempting just this type of educational program with its SoundByting campaign (**www.soundbyting.com**), which is targeting university administrators and students.

Unfortunately, there will probably always be people who take advantage of legitimate technologies for illegitimate purposes. It does seem that the Internet has made it easier to do so, and more "regular" people who wouldn't think of stealing a CD from a store will download the same CD from the Web without paying for it. Perhaps some people feel that because they aren't actually taking a physical object, they aren't hurting anyone—therefore, they are bending rather than breaking the law. However, although the risk of being caught is probably small as long as the person isn't redistributing illegal copies, these people are hurting others and violating U.S. copyright law.

What is copyright?

Copyright law is specified in Title 17 of the U.S. Code (federal law) and is intended to protect creators of original works, such as literary, dramatic, and musical works, by giving them exclusive rights to several actions, including the following:

▶ Reproduction and distribution of the work

▶ Public performance and display of the work

▶ Modification of the work to create derivative versions

The author of the work may authorize others to take these actions. Although there are some important limitations to the preceding rights, such as the doctrine of fair use, it is generally illegal for a person other than the copyright owner to take any of these actions without authorization. Anyone who violates these rights of the copyright owner can be subject to criminal penalties as specified by the law.

Copyright protection exists automatically after a work is created in a fixed form, and since 1989, no copyright notice on the work is required. For works created in 1978 or later, the protection is 70 years past the author's death; for works created anonymously, pseudonymously, or for hire in 1978 or later, the copyright term is the shorter of 95 years from the first publication or 120 years from creation.

The U.S. Copyright Office operates a Web site at **lcweb.loc.gov/copyright**, and this is a good place to learn more about copyright law.

Downloading and listening to MP3 files is perfectly legal, provided that the distributor has made the appropriate licensing arrangements with the copyright owners. Sites such as EMusic.com and MP3.com that sell MP3 files or offer them for free download have made these arrangements. (We'll discuss a number of Web sites where you can find legal MP3 downloads in **Section 2**.) It is also legal to create MP3 files from music CDs or other original media you already own. You can make as many copies of your music as you like for your own personal, noncommercial use, but you cannot give copies to your friends unless the copyright owner has specifically given that right (such as by putting the music in the public domain).

Willfully infringing copyright law by downloading unauthorized MP3s, however, might make you liable for criminal penalties under the No Electronic Theft *(NET)* Act if you are caught.

> **TIP**
>
> BitLaw (**www.bitlaw.com**) and nolo.com (**www.nolo.com**) are two good Web sites that offer copyright law information for the non-lawyer. Many people consider the book *Kohn on Music Licensing* to be indispensable for music-related law, and there is a Web site with related information at **www.kohnmusic.com**.

Copyright law forbids distribution of copies of copyrighted material without permission of the owner, even if you give it away for free, for trade, or do it in a way that promotes the material. However, for some very limited exceptions, see **Question 22**, "What is 'fair use'?"

> **TIP**
>
> Many bands, including The Grateful Dead, Phish, and the Dave Matthews Band, have allowed and even encouraged fans to tape their live performances. Typically, tapers may trade or give away copies to other tapers as long as the tapes are for personal use and no money is being made. The Resources for Tape Traders (**www.resourcesfortapers.com**) Web site is a good place to meet other tapers, trade in a variety of formats including MP3, and to learn more about the subject. The site also includes a list put together by Kurt Andrew Kemp of bands that are known to have a taping policy. You can find that at **www.resourcesfortapers.com/resources/tapeband.html**.

Q21 Can I put MP3 files on my Web page?

Making MP3 files of copyrighted music available for unlimited distribution from a Web page is legal with authorization from the copyright owners. This might be simple if the MP3 files you want to distribute are of your own work and you still own the copyright or if the work is in the public domain. However, if this is not the situation, you have to contact and receive permission from the copyright owner to use each song you want to put on your homepage.

Actually, you will most likely have to contact more than one owner, as most music is covered by two copyrights. One copyright is for the *musical work*, the written musical notation, and lyrics. The right to reproduce and distribute a musical work is usually administered by the Harry Fox Agency (**www.nmpa.org**). Downloading a digital audio file is also considered a public performance, so you have to license the performance right from the organization that represents the composer and publisher of the work, usually ASCAP (**www.ascap.com**), BMI (**www.bmi.com**), or SESAC (**www.sesac.com**).

The second copyright is for the *sound recording*, which is the actual recording of a particular artist performing the musical work. The sound recording is usually owned by a record company, which is under no obligation to grant permission to use the recording and might charge as much as it likes if it does choose to grant permission.

However, there are a few situations, under the fair use doctrine of copyright law, where you can distribute small portions of copyrighted audio without first getting permission.

Q22 What is "fair use?"

Copyright law makes several limited provisions for copying without first obtaining permission from the copyright holder. These include situations where material is copied for the purposes of review or criticism, educational use, or news reporting. All these factors, specified in Section 107 of copyright law, are to be used in determining whether a particular situation qualifies as a *fair use:*

▶ The purpose and character of the use, including whether such use is of commercial nature or is for nonprofit educational purposes

▶ The nature of the copyrighted work

▶ The amount and substantiality of the portion used in relation to the copyrighted work as a whole

▶ The effect of the use upon the potential market for or value of the copyrighted work

For example, an excerpt of a song used in a review to illustrate a point would probably be considered fair use. The courts have also maintained that making additional copies of music already owned by an individual for personal use falls within the doctrine of fair use. However, dubbing portions of previous recordings into a new recording (sampling) would not typically fall under the heading of fair use and would require clearance from the owner of the original recording, as well as licensing of the underlying musical composition.

Fair use is rarely clear-cut, because the factors used to determine whether a particular use qualifies often conflict with one another. If you find yourself in a situation involving questionable interpretation of the fair use doctrine, you should consult a copyright attorney.

Q23 Can I legally copy my MP3 music onto more than one computer or device?

Consumers are allowed to make as many copies of their music as they want, as long as the copies are for their own personal, noncommercial use. Protection from copyright liability under these conditions is provided by copyright law's doctrine of fair use. In fact, the recent lawsuit brought by the RIAA against Diamond Multimedia (mentioned in **Chapter 2**) clarifies this interpretation of the law.

The lawsuit concerned Diamond Multimedia's Rio, a portable device that could play MP3 files downloaded from a computer, and interpretation of the Audio Home Recording Act of 1992 (AHRA). The AHRA added protections to copyright law for consumer copying of music for personal use using analog and digital audio recording devices. The AHRA also required manufacturers of these devices to include a copy protection scheme to prevent multiple generation copying from copies and including payment of a royalty for each device sold to offset music industry losses due to copying.

In the lawsuit, the RIAA tried to show that the Rio violated the AHRA because it did not incorporate the required copy protection scheme. However, a U.S. Court of Appeals determined that the Rio, as a computer peripheral, was not covered by the AHRA, because that law intentionally excluded computer equipment from being considered as a digital audio recording device. The court went on to support consumers' right to *space-shift* their music between devices, comparing this to the time-shifting of copyrighted television programs using VCRs, which is also allowed under the fair use doctrine of copyright law. Regarding this space-shifting, the court said, "Such copying is paradigmatic non-commercial personal use entirely consistent with the purposes of the Act."

http://www.muskalipman.com

> **NOTE**
> The full decision in the RIAA versus Diamond Multimedia case can be read at the homepage of the 9th Circuit U.S. Court of Appeals at **www.ce9.uscourts.gov/opinions**. The opinion was given in June 1999.

Q24 Can I legally convert my music CDs to MP3 format?

Copying music from a music CD to MP3 format, a process known as *ripping*, is not specifically addressed in copyright law. Because the courts have determined that copying for personal, noncommercial use is allowed under fair use provisions, it follows that this conversion is perfectly fine. Many see the space-shifting decision discussed in the previous question as further evidence of this right.

So, it is okay to rip CDs you own to MP3 format provided you don't share any copies, still own the original CD, and don't use the copies for commercial purposes like professional disc jockeying, commercial radio, or outright sale. (We'll cover how to rip your CDs in **Section 4**, "Creating Your Own MP3 Files.")

Q25 What laws pertain to streaming MP3s for a Net radio station?

Copyright law also covers Net radio stations that stream digital audio to listeners. The licensing of the reproduction, distribution, and public performance rights of the underlying music work (the notes and lyrics) is virtually the same as for downloadable MP3 files discussed earlier in this chapter.

However, the *Digital Millennium Copyright Act (DMCA)* of 1998 greatly simplifies the process of obtaining the license for the sound recording, usually owned by a record company. The DMCA makes a provision for a *statutory license* for sound recordings.

A statutory license allows a Net radio broadcaster to play music legally without first obtaining an individual license specifically for each song. A statutory license also means that the Net radio broadcaster is guaranteed access to the sound recording, whereas with a downloadable MP3 file, there is no guarantee that the copyright owner would agree.

To qualify for a statutory license, the Net radio broadcaster must follow certain conditions, including, but not limited to, the following:

▶ Limits on the number of songs from a particular artist or album played consecutively

▶ No advance announcements of song or artist playlists can be made

▶ Limits on duration and scheduling of programs that loop continuously or are repeated at a later time

▶ An obligation to try to keep the recipient from copying the transmission

The complete details for these and the other conditions for the statutory license can be found on the RIAA Web Licensing FAQ at **www.riaa.com/weblic/wl_faq.htm**

An application for a statutory license is provided at the Library of Congress Copyright Office Web site at **www.loc.gov/copyright/licensing**.

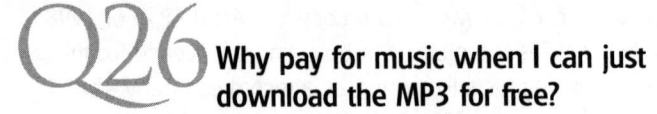

Q26: Why pay for music when I can just download the MP3 for free?

Just because it's easy to download pirated MP3s for free with little chance of being prosecuted doesn't mean you should do it. Besides being morally wrong and illegal, stealing music in this way hurts many people. Of course, it hurts the record companies, who, according to the RIAA, recover their investment on only 15 percent of recordings anyway and depend on those successes to support the rest of their artists and business. Digital audio piracy is also bad for retailers who sell music, whether it's in CD form or distributed legitimately using MP3 or another digital audio format, because it deprives them of sales. Piracy eventually hurts musicians and songwriters who depend on royalties they receive on sales of their work to earn a living.

Although some people use disenchantment with the music industry or the price of music as an excuse to pirate, there are better ways to change the system. For example, supporting artists and labels who do take advantage of legal digital audio distribution is one way to get the attention of the industry and still feel good about what you're doing. Besides, if we don't support musicians and songwriters today, who will be around to create great music tomorrow?

Section 2
Finding MP3 Music on the Web

4
Getting Access to MP3s

The Web can be a big place, and sometimes it's hard to figure out where to start when you're looking for something like MP3 music. This section will give you strategies for starting out and finding just what you're looking for. Actually, along the way you'll probably find more than you're looking for, but that's just the nature of the Web!

As you begin to discover the variety of MP3 music online, and the thousands of sites where MP3 is discussed and downloaded, you'll begin to see firsthand how the combination of MP3 and the Web are revolutionizing the music industry.

In the next few chapters, you'll find out about search engines and directories, places to get recommendations, where you can buy, where you can trade, and where you can download for free (legal or not). You'll also be introduced to a twist on MP3—streaming MP3 Net radio stations.

Getting Access to MP3s

Q27 What methods help me navigate to MP3s on the Internet?

The approach taken for finding MP3 files on the Web usually starts in one of two ways, depending on what you know about what you want. Following are the two navigation methods:

▶ Searching
▶ Browsing

Searching is the best approach to take when you have a definite idea of what MP3s you want, like tracks from a particular artist or a certain song. The searching approach can be compared to knowing exactly what CD you want to buy when you walk into a record store, asking the clerk to point out where it is, plucking it from its spot, and then walking right up to the checkout counter.

Browsing is a better way of finding MP3s when you aren't quite sure of what you're looking for. You might have some ideas, like the genre of music, but if you're browsing you probably don't have a specific artist or name of a song in mind. It's just like browsing at the record store and flipping through the CDs in the Jazz section; that's what you're in the mood for, but you don't have a particular choice.

Obviously, you don't usually use just one of these approaches at a time when you go shopping. Take the music store example: Even if you know exactly what album you want, as you're picking it out from the rack you probably flip through some of the other albums by the same artist, or perhaps something else nearby might catch your eye. Although there are MP3-related Web sites, notably MP3 search engines, that specialize in only one of the main types of navigation, the most useful sites incorporate browsing and searching with even more features. For example, a site might offer recommendations and reviews to help you find an artist you'd like.

Q28 What types of MP3-related sites are there?

There are a couple of main types of MP3-related sites that combine searching, browsing, and additional information (like music reviews and recommendations) in various combinations. As you become familiar with how these different types of sites are most useful, you'll probably use some of each kind. The three main site formats are the following:

- MP3 *portals*, or communities
- MP3 list sites
- MP3 search engines

A portal is a Web site that serves as a starting point to the Web, so an MP3 portal is a site that provides a view to everything MP3. They might include anything from links to download MP3 software, reviews of the latest portable MP3 players, and, of course, links to lots and lots of free MP3 tracks. These Web sites are often very artist friendly and might allow bands to set up a page describing themselves along with samples of their music. MP3.com, shown in **Figure 4.1**, is perhaps the best known MP3 portal site on the Web. MP3 portals often take a commercial approach, where some sample tracks from each album are free, but most are for purchase. A number of MP3 portal sites are described in depth in **Question 32**.

Figure 4.1 MP3.com is a major MP3 portal site.

MP3.com Services for Artists

MP3.com, which is one of the most popular music-related sites on the Web, attracts more than half a million visitors each day. It's always been a very artist-friendly site (more than 50,000 artists have music on MP3.com), and the company is actively trying to make itself even more attractive to new artists by integrating more features than just MP3 download capabilities. For example, MP3.com is establishing a strong relationship with **seeUthere.com**, a Web-based event planning site that provides services like automated invitations and online ticketing. MP3.com artists may soon be able to promote, manage, and book events all from the MP3.com site—showing that there's more than just MP3s offered at many MP3 portal sites.

Although the major MP3 portal sites are strictly playing the legal side of the MP3 game, another type of site often covers the smorgasbord of illegal MP3 files available on the Web. MP3 *list sites*, like the site shown in **Figure 4.2**, provide links to other Web sites with MP3 downloads. Virtually anything on the top charts around the world, and even complete albums, are available on these sites. However, you might have to wade through a sea of pop-up banner ads, browser windows, and even pornography to get to the actual links to the MP3s themselves. This availability of hit tracks for free represents a side of the MP3 revolution that has both driven the success of the format and drawn the ire of the music industry. List sites are discussed further in **Question 33**.

Figure 4.2 The MP3 Corner (**www.mp3corner.net**) list site provides links to other Web sites with MP3 downloads.

Several Web search engines specialized for MP3 files are available that attempt to give you a listing of MP3 files anywhere on the Web that match your search criteria. Lycos MP3 Search, shown in **Figure 4.3**, is a good example. Although these search engines can give you a long list of results, they often aren't the most efficient way to find MP3 files, because many links are outdated and point to files that no longer exist at that address. Also, an MP3 search engine that covers the whole Web does not tell you whether an MP3 file that shows up in your search results is being offered legally. In **Question 34**, you'll learn about several other MP3-specific Web search engines.

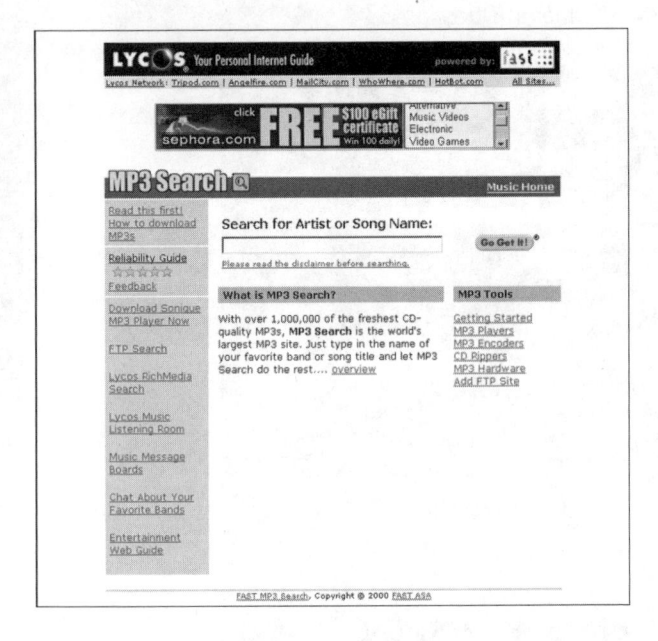

Figure 4.3 Lycos's MP3 Search lets you search the Web for MP3 music.

Q29 Don't I need a really fast connection to the Web to get MP3 files?

Even though they're compressed, MP3 files still take up quite a bit of space. Having a slower connection isn't usually a problem, but you'll have to wait longer for your downloads to finish. Your MP3 experience will likely be more enjoyable if you have a fast connection.

Table 4.1 provides some estimated download times for a four-minute MP3 file that takes up about 4MB of space. However, you should be aware that you often won't get the maximum speed from any of these types of connections. Networks are a lot like roads—things can slow down for everyone when there's lots of traffic. Your Internet service provider should be able to tell you what the peak usage times are so you can avoid them if you wish. If the non-peak times are inconvenient for you, one option is to try a download scheduling utility (see **Question 31** on scheduling downloads). Your download speeds can also be affected by the network serving the site you're trying to download from. To use the road analogy again—it doesn't matter if the way home is a speedy four-lane highway if you have to wait in line to get out of the parking lot.

Choosing a server for your MP3s

If you create some MP3s of music you've written or performed and are thinking of setting up a homepage to serve the music up for your fans, you'll want to keep the issue of network capacity in mind. Choosing a hosting service (like MP3.com or another MP3 artist community site) that is intended to handle lots of traffic will help prevent frustration for those people who try to download *your* music. **Chapter 13**, "Distributing Your Own Music Using MP3," has more tips on this subject.

Table 4.1—Expected Download Times

Expected download times for a four-minute MP3 track (about 4MB). The speed you actually get may be less depending on network traffic and your ISP.

Access Type	Typical Speed	Approximate Download Time
Standard Modem	28.8-56Kbps	10-20 min.
ISDN	128Kbps	4-5 min.
DSL	784+Kbps	1 min. or less
Cable Modem	1+Mbps	1 min. or less

If you have a regular modem and find you aren't content with it, you can read on to the next question for some tips, or you might want to investigate some higher-speed options.

Getting Access to MP3s - Chapter 4

> **TIP**
> You can learn more about high-speed Internet connections using DSL and cable modems by contacting your local phone or cable companies or by checking out one of these Web sites:
>
> **DSL**
> 2Wire: DSL availability lookup and tutorial **www.2wire.com/dsllookup/finddsl.asp** DSL Reports: Information and service reviews **www.dslreports.com**
>
> **Cable Modems**
> Cable-Modems.Org: Tutorial and resources on cable modems **www.cable-modems.org**

Q30 What are performance tips for regular home modem users?

What if you don't subscribe to a high-speed Internet service like *DSL* or *cable modem* and find that you just don't have the patience to wait for MP3 files to download? Here are a few ways you can make your MP3 finding a bit more enjoyable:

▶ Optimize Windows modem settings
▶ Listen to streaming audio
▶ Purchase MP3s on CD-ROM

Optimize Windows Modem Settings

If you're using Windows 95, 98, or NT as your computer's operating system, it's quite possible you're not getting the maximum performance from your network or modem connection. Windows has several settings that are hidden away in the Registry that affect the efficiency of data transfer between your modem and your ISP. A utility such as TweakDUN, from Patterson Designs, is the easiest way to experiment with and change these settings to get the best download times (see **Figure 4.4**). (If you'd like the full-blown technical explanation of how TweakDUN works, check out the FAQ on their Web site.) Using this utility will involve some time to read the suggested procedures and experiment with the combinations of settings, but it can pay off if you get faster downloads as a result. Reviewers have reported download speed being increased by 40 percent in some cases, though there's no guarantee that you'll see the same improvement, since it depends on the combination of your computer and your ISP.

TweakDUN costs $15, and a limited trial version can be downloaded for free from the Patterson Designs Web site at **www.pattersondesigns.com/tweakdun/**.

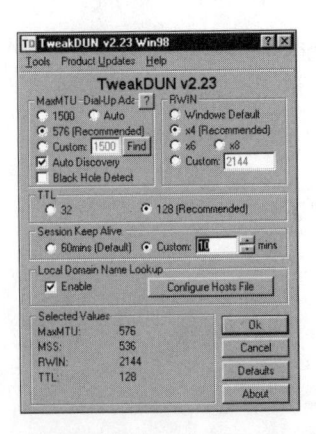

Figure 4.4 Using the TweakDUN utility can improve network performance for Windows.

Streaming Audio

Another option for those who can't wait for a regular MP3 download is *streaming audio*. Streaming audio is played from a server in a constant feed, so you can listen as you go rather than wait for an entire file to be downloaded. If a regular MP3 file is comparable to a CD track, streaming audio might be compared to listening to a radio station. Streaming audio might be provided from the server on demand when you request it, or it might be continuously broadcast, which is commonly known as *Net radio*. Streaming audio often uses MP3 compression, although there are other formats such as the popular RealAudio that use different, proprietary compression methods. Streaming audio is discussed in depth in **Chapter 8**, "Net Radio—Streaming MP3."

Buy MP3 on CD-ROM

Another option for users who don't want to download MP3 tracks is to purchase them on a CD-ROM. For example, MP3.com offers what it calls *DAM CDs* for many of the bands it represents. DAM CDs contain MP3 tracks that can be read when the disc is placed in a CD-ROM drive, as well as the songs in regular CD audio format, so the disc can be played in your CD player. We'll cover shopping for MP3 files in more depth in **Chapter 6**, "Buying MP3 Tracks."

Opportunities for purchasing MP3s on CD-ROM are fairly limited, because most people prefer to download the MP3 file directly. You might want to read more in **chapters 10** and **11** to find out how to create MP3 files from the more easily purchased regular music CDs.

Q31 How can I schedule my MP3 downloads?

Download scheduling utilities let you set up a series of downloads for a more convenient time, such as overnight. This can be especially useful if you are sharing a phone line for regular voice communication. Here are two examples of these useful programs:

Netzip Download Demon (www.downloaddemon.com)

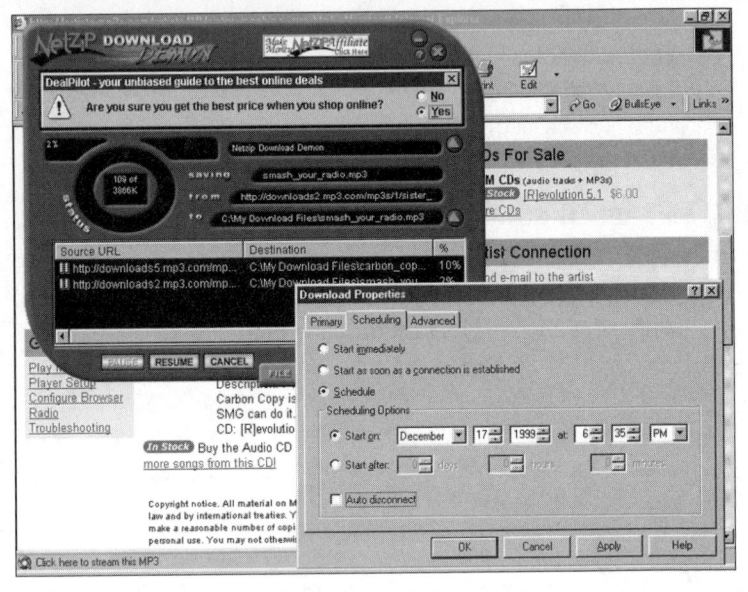

Figure 4.5 Netzip Download Demon allows you to schedule your downloads.

Download Demon, shown in **Figure 4.5,** is a free utility that intercepts downloads from your Netscape or Internet Explorer browser when you click on a link to an MP3 (or any other file to be downloaded). It then allows you to control your downloads by pausing and restarting them. It also allows you to resume a download if you get disconnected from the server or from your ISP. The Scheduling feature allows you to set a future time that you want to resume downloading your files.

Headlight Software GetRight (www.getright.com)

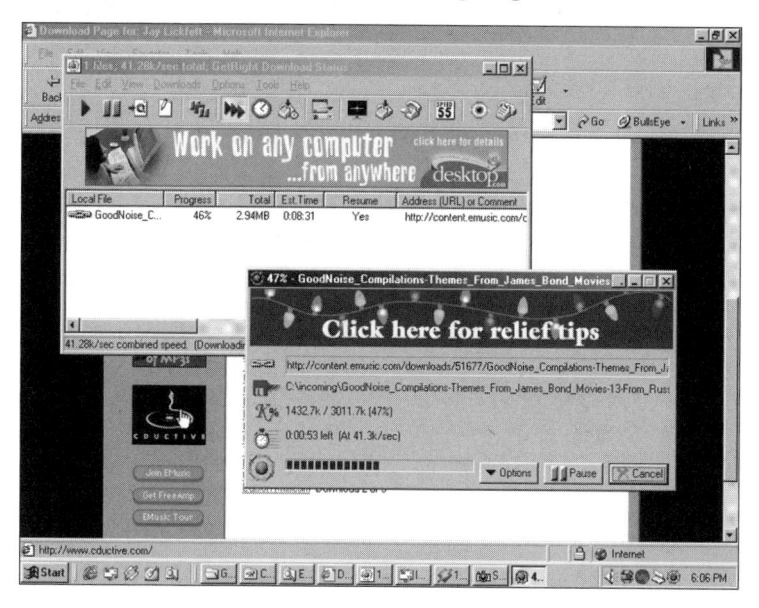

Figure 4.6 Using Headlight Software GetRight to control a download.

GetRight, shown in **Figure 4.6,** is another highly rated download utility. Besides options for scheduling downloads, it can resume disconnected downloads, even redialing your ISP if necessary. It intercepts links to files you click on in your Web browser, or you can drag and drop the links right to the GetRight program to add them to the list. GetRight can even show you a list of all the links on a page so you can choose which ones you want to download. GetRight costs $20, but an evaluation version can be downloaded free from its Web site.

5

Using MP3 Portals, List Sites, and Search Engines

Q32 What are some good MP3 portals and communities?

MP3 portal sites are often the best place to start looking for MP3 files on the Web. Not only can you rest assured that the tracks you download from these sites are being legally distributed, they also have reliable availability. Portals usually allow you to browse or search, and they often include music news, reviews, tutorials for MP3 software and devices, message boards, and more. A number of popular MP3 portal sites are compared in **Table 5.1**.

Table 5.1—Features of some popular MP3 portal sites

	MP3.com	Change Music Network	MP3now.com	EMusic	IUMA	Rolling Stone.com	ARTIST direct network	RioPort	Listen.com
Search Site and/or Web for MP3s	X	X	X	X	X	X	X	X	X
Browse the Site for MP3s	X	X		X	X	X	X	X	X
Types of Artists Included in Site:									
Well Known	X			X		X	X	X	X
Less-Well Known	X	X		X	X	X	X	X	X
Music and Artist Reviews	X	X	X			X	X		X
Personalized Recommendations	X								
Message Boards and/or Chat	X		X		X	X		X	X
Artists Can Create a Homepage & Submit MP3s	X	X			X	X	X		
Music and MP3 Related News	X		X	X		X	X	X	
MP3 Software/ Hardware Reviews	X		X						
MP3 Tutorials	X	X	X						X

MP3.com (www.MP3.com)

MP3.com, shown in **Figure 5.1**, is one of the leading destinations on the Web for MP3-related resources, including digital audio news, reviews of MP3 software and hardware, and tutorials, not to mention a collection of more than 400,000 free MP3 tracks from more than 65,000 independent artists. Independent artists are encouraged to create their own homepages on the MP3.com site and post sample downloads of their music. MP3.com also occasionally features promotional tracks from well-known artists such as Alanis Morissette and the Eagles.

MP3.com includes a number of features that make it stand out from the other MP3 portal sites. The site offers personalized recommendations of music for you to try based on other tracks you've listened to on previous visits to the site. Another feature, called Stations, allows anyone to create a homepage within the MP3.com site and incorporate any of the tracks in the MP3.com collection. Many people have used this to set up topical or regional interest pages as well as digital audio e-zines. MP3.com also sells DAM CDs, which are single discs that contain both audio tracks and MP3 tracks. **Chapter 6** discusses buying MP3 tracks, including DAM CDs, in more depth.

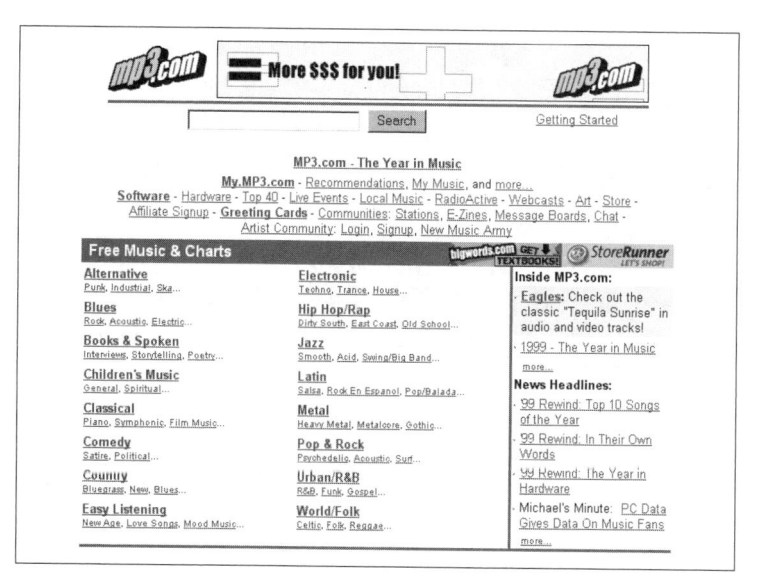

Figure 5.1 MP3.com is an excellent place to start your MP3 hunt.

Change Music Network (www.changemusic.com)

The Change Music Network is dedicated to helping independent artists take advantage of digital audio for sharing and selling their music, and it's another good place to find free MP3s (see **Figure 5.2**). Its main site includes featured tracks, browsing and searching of the many homepages set up by bands, as well as message boards. The site also links to several other MP3 portal sites that are a part of the Change Music Network, including MP3now, which is described next.

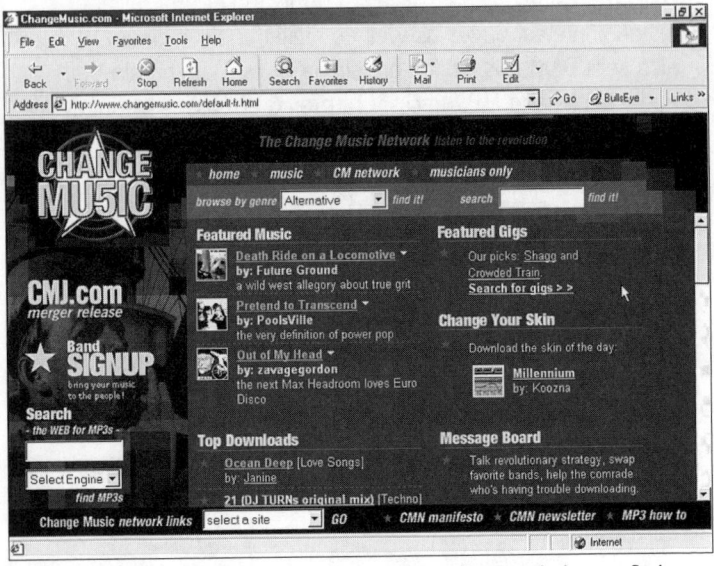

Figure 5.2 The Change Music Network site is another good place to find MP3 samples of independent artists.

Using MP3 Portals, List Sites, and Search Engines - Chapter 5

MP3now (www.mp3now.com)

As you can see in **Figure 5.3**, MP3now has one of the best collections of MP3-related information and lots of links to other information spread across the Web. It includes links to recent digital audio news stories, as well as featured artists on the Change Music Network. MP3now includes a good listing of MP3 search engines.

Figure 5.3 MP3now has a great offering of MP3-related news, reviews, and tutorials.

EMusic (www.emusic.com)

The EMusic portal, shown in **Figure 5.4**, includes digital audio news and some limited MP3 tutorials, but it's best for its large selection of MP3 tracks available for purchase. At the EMusic site, you can browse the catalog of independent and well-known artists' tracks, listen to sample clips, and purchase individual tracks or entire albums to download.

Figure 5.4 EMusic sells downloadable MP3 tracks.

Internet Underground Music Archive (IUMA) (www.iuma.com)

IUMA is one of the longest running Internet sites for helping independent musicians promote themselves, making it a good place to discover new groups and sample their music (see **Figure 5.5**). Bands build custom homepages within IUMA with band info, MP3 downloads, and message boards where fans can respond. You can also purchase music CDs through IUMA from some of the bands.

Figure 5.5 IUMA is another place to find music from independent artists.

RollingStone.com (www.rollingstone.com)

RollingStone.com is a great site that covers all aspects of the popular music world, with a heavy dose of digital audio content, including MP3. The MP3 & More portion of the site gives bands a place to set up their own promotional page with downloadable tracks in MP3 or other formats. Check out the editors' picks to see what they liked best or browse through the bands yourself. One of the best parts of the RollingStone.com site is the "search by influence" feature, which lets you find bands that have listed groups that have influenced their work. This can often help find music that matches your tastes much more easily. The site also offers promotional downloads from many well-known groups in MP3 and other digital audio formats. RollingStone.com is shown in **Figure 5.6**.

Figure 5.6 RollingStone.com's MP3 & More has promotional downloads from big-name artists as well as independent artists.

Using MP3 Portals, List Sites, and Search Engines - Chapter 5

Figure 5.6 continued

BUY
MP3s
GIFTS
CDs CDNOW

MAGAZINE SERVICES
SUBSCRIBE
BACK ISSUES
ADDRESS CHANGE
TEMPORARY HOLD
DELIVERY PROBLEMS

E-mail groups:
Metal [GO]
globelists.com

EMAIL OUR EDITORS
CONTACT US
RS EVENTS
STEAL OUR SITES
MEDIA KIT
EMAIL THIS URL

RollingStone.com
Millennium
Gift
Guide

SPECIAL OFFERS
COMPARISON SHOP AT MYSIMON.COM!

VISA: GET IT ONLINE, USE IT EVERYWHERE!

GET BLUE FROM AMERICAN EXPRESS

CLICK HERE for high school photos of CELEBS.

Moby
Bodyrock
Dance & DJ

Anthony Anderson
Number 33
Alternative

The Spinatras
Michelle
Alternative

ROLLING STONE EDITORS' PICKS

1	Frank Foster	Gray Thursday	
	Jazz		
	Editors' Rating: 6.20		
2	Verb & Marquis — Rap & Hip Hop	Where Da Party At? (Explicit)	5.8
3	Weak Lazy Liar — New Age	Bright Yellow Bucket	5.6
4	Violet Scene — Alternative	For a Second	5.4
5	Octavian Peagu — Classical & Opera	I'll Provide	5.25
6	I-Brow — Dance & DJ	Circular Motions (I-Brow Mix)	5.2
7	Woolworthy — Alternative	Leap Year	5.2
8	Method Engine — Alternative	Crutch	5
9	Mingo — R&B & Soul	Got the Fix	5
10	Robert West — Alternative	A Pizza Is Me Guy	4.8
11	SugarBuzz — Rap & Hip Hop	Buzz Envy	4.8

The editors are: Nathan Brackett, Jason Fine, Mark Healy, Matt Hendrickson and Joe Levy

Editors' Picks archive

NEW TRACKS

1	Amy Abdou	Invisible Armies
2	Chyl Da Most Hated	Kentucky Skunk radio
3	Chyl Da Most Hated	Ghetto Love radio
4	Grapevine	I'm Awake
5	Grapevine	Comfortable
6	1 Five Da Crime Family	Gunsmoke
7	1 Five Da Crime Family	Drug Sniffin' K9
8	EXIT 99	The Freshman
9	EXIT 99	The Purpose
10	EXIT 99	Ronco's Wonderland

more new tracks

[EMAIL TO FRIEND]

[ALL ACCESS ▼]

Section 2 Finding MP3 Music

http://www.muskalipman.com

ARTISTdirect network (www.artistdirect.com)

The ARTISTdirect network is another general music portal that includes a lot of free digital audio downloads (see **Figure 5.7**). The network is made up of several main sites, including the Ultimate Band List (UBL), iMusic, and DOWNLOADSdirect. These sites offer a specialized Web search engine for music-related content, official Web sites for many well-known groups, message boards and chat, music downloads from major artists, and tracks uploaded by independent bands. The site also includes an online store where you can order music CDs and other music-related merchandise and collectibles.

Figure 5.7 The ARTISTdirect network is another great general music resource that includes MP3 downloads.

RioPort (www.rioport.com)

RioPort is another good place to find MP3 and other digital audio files for free or for purchase. The site was created by Diamond Multimedia, makers of the Rio portable MP3 player, hence the name, RioPort. As shown in **Figure 5.8**, there's a wide variety of music at the site, much of it from well-known artists, as well as spoken works such as biographies, history, fiction, training and educational programs, and poetry. RioPort has an agreement with Universal Music Group to distribute music from the group's labels (Universal, MCA, Geffen, and others) beginning in late 1999, but most of this will be provided in formats other than MP3.

Figure 5.8 RioPort has a large selection of digital audio downloads.

http://www.muskalipman.com

Listen.com (www.listen.com)

You might think of the Listen.com site (see **Figure 5.9**) as the ultimate directory of downloadable MP3s. This site's goal is to include links to as many legal MP3 files as possible, including MP3s that are being distributed from other portal sites like EMusic.com and MP3.com. Because it is careful not to include illegally copied MP3s in the directory, Listen.com has been praised by, and has even attracted investments from, the music industry.

Listen.com provides a summary of each artist, and visitors to the site can add their own thoughts and ratings for the artists. The site's directory includes what site actually has the track, whether the track is free, and a link to a sample clip for many tracks, in addition to the link to the MP3 itself.

Figure 5.9 The Listen.com directory includes an artist summary, links to tracks, and member comments.

Q33 What are some examples of MP3 list sites?

No one denies that the availability of lots of popular music in MP3 format has contributed greatly to the success of the MP3 movement. The fact that most of the tracks from the top charts that are available in MP3 are being distributed without the permission of the owner has not been much of a hindrance to this trend, much to the dismay of many artists and record companies.

MP3 list sites are one way these illegal MP3 files are often organized. (There *are* list sites that point to legitimately distributed MP3s; however, most do not.) An MP3 list site doesn't actually store MP3 files. Instead, it provides links to other sites with the MP3s, which disappear and reappear at a different Web URL on a regular basis as they are shut down and another site is started. Many list sites have links to all the most recent hits, as well as full albums of popular artists that have been ripped from CDs and turned into MP3 files.

There are problems with MP3 list sites beyond the fact that they are often linking to illegally copied tracks. List sites are typically supported by selling advertising and can pop up a dozen or more new browser windows of ads when you click on links. Links are often broken, and when they *are* working, the server hosting the actual MP3 file might be quite slow.

> **TIP**
> Many list sites imply that it's legal to download the MP3 files they list as long as you delete them within a short time, typically 24 hours. This is not true—copying and distributing music without permission of the owner is illegal regardless of how long the copy is kept. Refer to **Chapter 3**, "MP3 and the Law," for more on the legal issues raised by MP3.

Here are several examples of MP3 list sites:

▶ Top 25 MP3 Sites (**www.top25mp3.com**) (see **Figure 5.10**)
▶ Free MP3 Files (**www.free-mp3-files.com**)
▶ The MP3 Resource (**www.mp3-resource.net**)

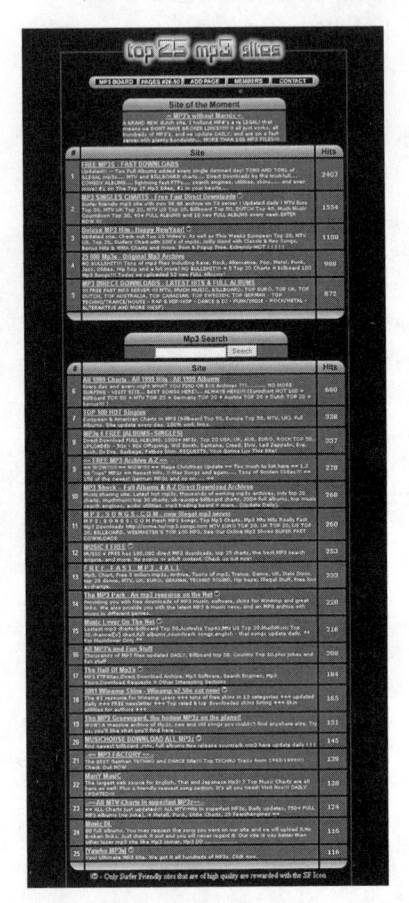

Figure 5.10 Top 25 MP3 Sites: A typical MP3 list site.

Q34 — What are some MP3 search engine sites?

If you know what you want, Internet MP3 *search engines* can be a great way to find a certain song or music by a particular artist. These search sites are slightly different than the search functionality provided by many MP3 portal sites, because they provide results from the Internet rather than just the contents of one site. Internet MP3 search sites build an index of links to MP3 files from many locations all over the Internet. You can type in keywords from the title of a song or the name of a band and get a list of links to the file that the search engine has previously discovered. MP3 search engines are similar to general Web search engines like AltaVista and Google, but they specialize in MP3 files so that you don't get a lot of extraneous hits in your results listing.

Unfortunately, an MP3 search engine can't tell the difference between a site distributing legal MP3 files and one distributing illegal files. So, a large number of the results provided by MP3 search engines are links to pirated MP3 files.

> **TIP**
> Many results returned by MP3 search engines are links to sites that enforce upload/download ratios. The idea is that you have to give them a certain number of MP3 files from your collection before they will let you download any of theirs. You must use a real *FTP* client, such as CuteFTP (**www.cuteftp.com**), to access these *ratio sites*. There is an excellent tutorial on using FTP to download MP3 tracks at the Palavista MP3 search site at: **www.palavista.com/information/download.shtml**

Popular MP3 search engines include the following:

▶ **AudioFind (www.audiofind.com)**
An excellent search site that also provides direct links to results of recently popular search queries (see **Figure 5.11**). The site also includes an index of its links browsable by title and artist name.

▶ **Lycos MP3 Search (mp3.lycos.com)**
Lycos is a major search engine for many topics, but this portion of the site is specifically for MP3 music.

▶ **MP3Board.com (www.mp3board.com)**
A good search site that also lets you browse by genre. The site also features lots of links to MP3 list sites.

▶ **2Look4 (www.2look4.com)**
This site has a simple interface with several options for filtering results according to their reliability and whether they have download/upload ratios.

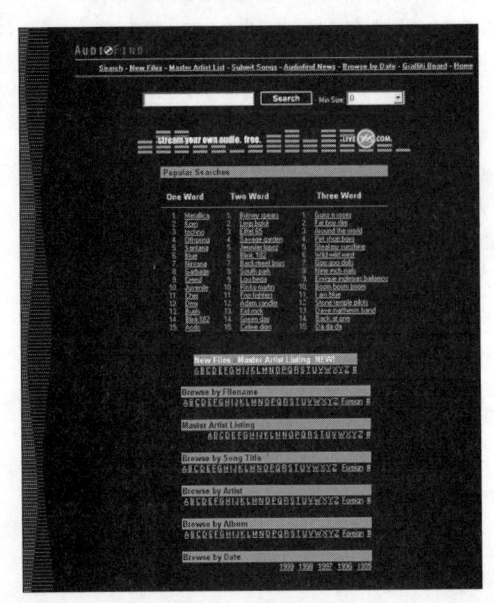

Figure 5.11 AudioFind is a good example of an MP3 search engine site.

> **TIP**
> Many MP3 portal sites maintain a list of MP3 search engines. MP3now keeps one such listing here:
> **www.mp3now.com/html/mp3_search.html**

Q35 Can you help me find specific music I want?

Each search engine site has a slightly different way of processing the query terms you give it, so it's best to give the site's help page a quick read. However, there are a few general hints that can help you find what you're looking for faster.

▶ **Leave out meaningless and common words**
Words like *and* and *the* are so common that they don't help your search at all. Many search engines strip them out automatically, but it doesn't hurt to leave them out yourself when entering the query.

▶ **Be as specific as possible**
When entering your search query, use more than one keyword. Be as specific as you can and you'll get far more targeted results. You can always make your search more broad if you don't get any hits the first time. For example, let's say you're a tape trader and are trying to find a recording of a live performance of the song "Ants Marching" by the Dave Matthews Band. An efficient search might include the following keywords: *live Dave Matthews Ants Marching*. By using several words, you can quickly eliminate songs that include some of these terms but aren't what you're really after.

▶ **Take advantage of unusual words or spellings**
Unusual spellings and uncommon words in songs or band names can quickly get you to just what you want if you use them as your search query.

For example, perhaps now you're looking for another live recording of the Dave Matthews Band—"All Along the Watchtower." The words *all, along,* and *the* aren't very distinctive, but *Watchtower* is more unusual. An efficient search for this track might include the following terms: *live Dave Matthews Watchtower.*

Q36 I get a lot of results when I search, but none of the links are good. How come?

Results from MP3 search engines often include many links that don't appear to work. Many times, this is because the MP3 file no longer exists at that location. The site owner might have moved the files around, turned off the computer, or even had the site shut down by a system administrator. Some search engines provide a reliability rating along with each link, but even this isn't a guarantee that the links will be good.

If you click on a link to what you think is an MP3 file and nothing happens, there are still a few tricks you can try.

First, try right-clicking on the link, rather than just following it directly. Choose Save Link As or Save Target As to save the file to your computer. When you do this, the file might not have an .MP3 file extension. Many times, MP3 files are renamed with a different extension to try to hide them (from system administrators, for example). Many MP3 search engines can determine that the file is actually an MP3 file, so it is still listed as a result when you search. Simply rename the file after you download it so it will work with your MP3 player.

If this doesn't work, the site might be a ratio site, which means you have to trade MP3s to get access to download. Ratio sites and how to deal with them are discussed in the tip on page 77..

If you have to jump through any of these hoops to download an MP3 file, it's a pretty sure bet it's coming from an illegal archive, as they tend to be much less reliable than legitimate sources of MP3 files. You might want to try checking one of the MP3 portal sites discussed earlier to find a legal distributor of the track. Another option is to buy the music CD and convert it to MP3 format for your own use. Creating MP3s from a music CD is discussed in **Chapter 12**.

Q37 Is there a way to search multiple MP3 sites all at once, so I don't have to enter the same query into each one?

One way to speed up searching the Web for MP3 files is to use a meta-search site. These are Web sites that look like MP3 search engines but behind the scenes are quite different. Whereas MP3 search engines each build their own index of links to MP3 files that they find on the Internet, a *meta-search engine* doesn't try to find MP3s and doesn't build an index. Instead, it sends your query on to several MP3 search engines and collects *their* results. It then combines all the results returned from the various search engines and shows you all of them in one listing.

Following are a few popular meta-search engines:

▶ Palavista (www.palavista.com)

▶ SeekMP3.com (www.seekmp3.com)

▶ cybertropix (www.cybertropix.com)

> **TIP**
> Although meta-search sites can help you cover territory faster, they usually cannot include special features that individual MP3 search engine sites have, such as filtering, reliability ratings, or browsable indexes.

Q38 How can I find artists and music I like so I don't spend a lot of time downloading music I think is terrible?

This is a tough one, because everyone's tastes vary. There are, however, some ways to cut out things you know you'll dislike. As it turns out, the best ways to find new artists you like in MP3 format are probably very similar to the ways you find out about new CDs. Try the following:

▶ **Listen to the radio**
Listening to Net radio stations is a way of finding new bands and music you like. Check out **Chapter 8**, "Net Radio— Streaming MP3," for more on this aspect of the MP3 world.

▶ **Band/music reviews and discussion**
Many of the MP3 portal sites discussed earlier in this chapter include reviews or featured MP3 tracks selected by the editors, as well as comments and discussion by other listeners on message boards or chat. Taking a look and participating in these can be a great way to find new bands that match your tastes.

▶ **Sample clips**
Before you buy that MP3 track and download it, trying the sample clips is a relatively quick way to see if you think you'll like the music. Sample clips can come in a couple of different forms—small downloadable files, or as an MP3 stream (audio that can be played at the same time it is being downloaded—see **Chapter 8**). For example, you can download a thirty-second-long sample for most tracks

available at EMusic.com. If the complete song is four minutes long, you can get the sample in about one-eighth the time of downloading the whole track (plus, the sample is free). MP3.com is an example of a site that takes the streaming approach to samples. It offers a Lo Fi choice for users with modems and a Hi Fi choice if you have a fast connection to the Internet. The big advantage of streaming samples is that you don't have to wait at all to hear the clip.

Q39 What is Napster?

Napster (**www.napster.com**) combines a lot of features of MP3 portals, list sites, and search engines, but rather than being a Web site, it's a program you install on your computer. Using the Napster program, you can share your MP3 collection and chat with other people logged on to Napster and download MP3s from other Napster users. The idea is that communities can form to support independent artists distributing their music as MP3 files. However, the Napster software makes no determination about which files on a user's computer can be legally distributed and which can't.

With Napster, it's easy to share MP3 music with others, and at any given time during the day, there are hundreds of thousands of MP3 tracks available through the tool. Using Napster to find music is also often much faster than using a list site or a search engine because the program only displays MP3 tracks that are currently available.

Widespread use of Napster to share copyrighted music caught the attention of the RIAA, which sued the company for contributory copyright infringement in December 1999. By February 2000, Napster had become so popular that some universities had to resort to blocking access to the service because students using it to trade MP3 files were consuming substantial portions (in some cases, 40 percent or more) of the schools' network capacity. At the time of this writing, the RIAA's lawsuit against Napster had not been resolved.

6
Buying MP3 Tracks

Q40 Where can I buy MP3 tracks online?

Two Web sites—Emusic.com and MP3.com—dominate the legal MP3-for-purchase landscape, and each takes a slightly different approach for actually getting the MP3 to you.

EMusic.com (www.emusic.com)

EMusic has been a huge proponent of the MP3 format and is one of the leading sites on the Web for purchasing MP3s. It has been a pioneer in providing downloadable music in the MP3 format since the company was founded in early 1998.

EMusic works with independent record labels, as well as directly with artists, to license its tracks, and it boasts tens of thousands of tracks available for purchase and download. EMusic covers the whole range of music genres and offers tracks from a number of top artists in each genre, as well as many lesser known groups (see **Figure 6.1**).

You can browse the EMusic site, listening to sample clips of the tracks that are for sale, and find entire tracks occasionally offered for free. Additional tracks can be purchased on an individual basis for 99 cents each; all the tracks on a given album can be downloaded for $8.99.

86 Buying MP3 Tracks - Chapter 6

Figure 6.1 EMusic.com is the leading Web site for purchasing and downloading MP3 tracks and albums.

MP3.com (www.mp3.com)

Although most artists listed on the MP3.com directory generally provide most or all of their MP3s for free download, you can also purchase albums on an actual CD-ROM through MP3.com's DAM (Digital Automatic Music) program (see **Figure 6.2**). A DAM CD contains the tracks of the album in both MP3 format and standard CD audio format. That means you can read the MP3 files from it using your computer's MP3 player, or you can listen to the same songs using your regular CD player.

Artists who elect to participate in the DAM program split the proceeds of any albums they sell, and consumers get an actual disc shipped to them. Many DAM CDs sell for just $6.

http://www.MUSKALIPMAN.com

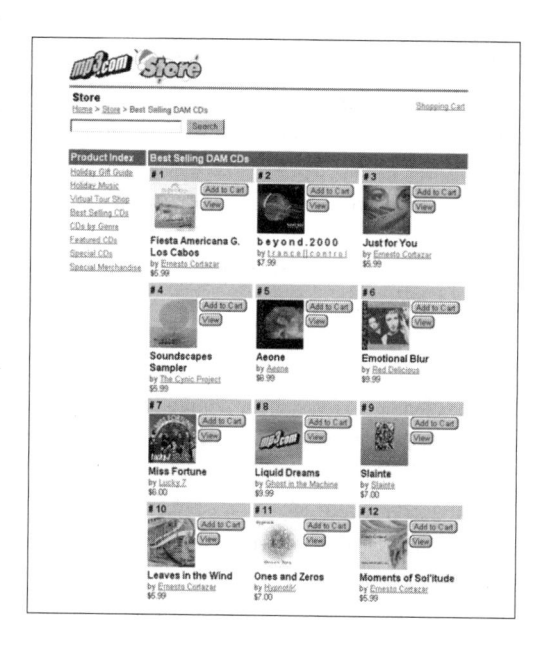

Figure 6.2 You can purchase DAM CDs from the MP3.com store at www.mp3.com/store.

EMusic.com and MP3.com aren't the only places you can buy and download MP3s. Other good Web sites to check out include:

MusicMaker (www.musicmaker.com)

At MusicMaker, you can select individual tracks from a large library of music (including music from the major label EMI) to create a custom music CD that will be shipped to you. Many of these tracks may also be purchased and downloaded as MP3, Windows Media Audio, or Liquid Audio files.

Mjuice.com (www.mjuice.com)

Mjuice sells tracks from many artists in an encrypted MP3 format. The *encryption* scheme used by Mjuice makes it harder for music pirates to copy the tracks illegally, but it also means that you must register at the Mjuice Web site and use an approved player to listen to the tracks. Winamp and RealJukebox are two players that support the Mjuice encrypted MP3 format.

Listen.com (www.listen.com)

Listen.com is a directory of digital audio files available on the Web. While you can't buy tracks at Listen.com, it's a great place to start because it links directly to the music being sold at other Web sites, including EMusic.com and MP3.com. For more on Listen.com, see **Question 32**, "What are some good MP3 portals and communities?"

Q41 What are the advantages of buying music in MP3 format?

One of the biggest advantages of buying music in MP3 format is convenience. You don't have to drive to the music store to buy an album if you can just download it from the comfort of your own home.

Buying MP3 tracks is also almost always less expensive than buying CDs, because you don't have to purchase tracks you don't like and the cost of an album is cheaper when you're not paying for a physical product. Even a DAM CD from MP3.com is cheaper than a typical music CD, because MP3.com has cut out many of the middle layers of the distribution chain.

Buying music already in MP3 format instead of a regular music CD also saves you the time it takes to convert the tracks to MP3—and with a DAM CD you still have the music CD there, too!

Q42 What are the disadvantages of buying music in MP3 format?

Someone with a slow Internet connection might argue that the convenience factor of MP3 is canceled out by the time it takes to download an album. However, by using a download scheduler utility, you can do other things while it downloads. Also, as faster Internet connections become more prevalent, this will be less and less an issue. For some handy tips that can make your MP3 downloads less of a hassle, see **Question 30**, "What are performance tips for regular home modem users?"

Another disadvantage of downloading MP3s instead of buying a CD is that you don't get a paper sleeve with cover art, lyrics, and band information. However, MP3 files can include pictures and text along with the audio by using an *ID3v2 tag*. Some MP3 players—like MusicMatch Jukebox—can read and display the information in these tags when they are included in an MP3 track. For more on ID3v2 tags and an older, more limited type of tag called ID3v1, see **Question 75**, "How can I set the track information that gets displayed by my MP3 player?" If you'd like to listen to the MP3s you buy using a regular CD player, you must use a CD-R drive and audio CD creation software to convert your MP3 tracks to the normal CD music format. Fortunately, this process is quite easy, as you'll see in **Chapter 12**, "How to Get the Most Out of Your MP3 Collection." However, if you plan to listen to your music on a standard CD player most of the time, it might be more convenient to buy the CD and convert tracks to MP3 rather than the other way around.

http://www.muskalipman.com

One of the biggest disadvantages of trying to buy your music in MP3 format is that not all music is available for legal purchase and download. Although some of the top artists are selling their albums in MP3 format, the major labels still have not accepted MP3. As a result, the selection of well-known artists just isn't the same as if you walked into a record store.

Q43 How do I buy an MP3 track?

Buying MP3s online is easy! To illustrate, here are the steps to buy several tracks by They Might Be Giants from the EMusic.com Web site.

▶ Point your browser to the EMusic.com Web site (**www.emusic.com**). Since we know the name of the artist we're looking for, we'll navigate using the Artist Index provided in the site's menu (see **Figure 6.3**).

Figure 6.3 The EMusic.com menu includes a link to the Artist Index.

▶ Using the Artist Index controls ❶, navigate until you find They Might Be Giants listed ❷ (see **Figure 6.4**). Click the band's name to go to the list of their available tracks.

Figure 6.4 Navigate the Artist Index to find the group you're looking for.

▶ At the They Might Be Giants page, follow the link for the album *Lincoln*.

▶ At the album page (see **Figure 6.5**) you can listen to sample clips ❶ and check off the tracks you'd like to purchase ❷. To add the songs you've selected to your shopping cart, click the Add To Cart button ❸ at the bottom of the page. If you'd like to purchase the entire album, you can simply click the Buy Whole Album button ❹.

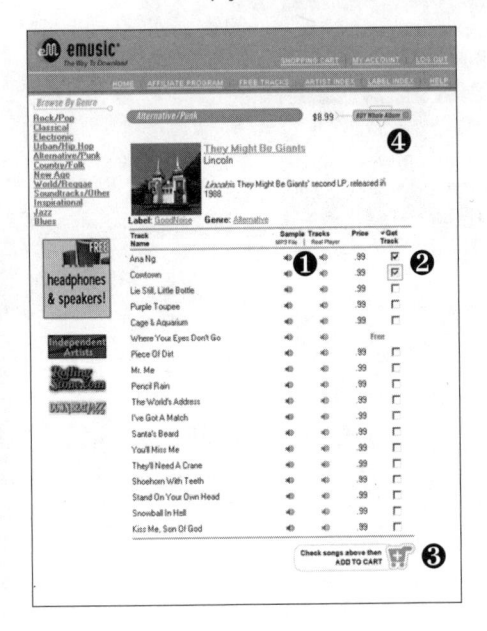

Figure 6.5 Listen to samples and choose tracks to order at the page for the album.

▶ The next screen you'll see (**Figure 6.6**) is your shopping cart—a listing of the tracks and/or entire albums you've selected ❶. You can click Continue Shopping ❷ to add more to your cart, or click Proceed to Checkout ❸.

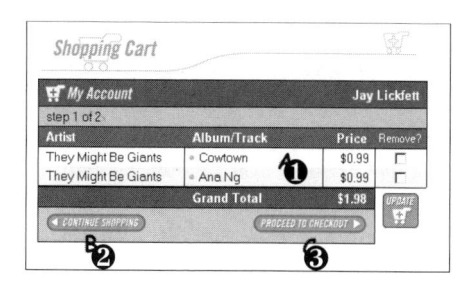

Figure 6.6 The shopping cart screen shows your selections.

▶ At this point, you need to log in (see **Figure 6.7**) using your EMusic.com account (❶ and ❷) if you've already set one up. If this is the first time you've bought from EMusic.com, you'll need to set up an account by clicking Create Account ❸. The Create Account form will ask for your shipping address and a credit card that you'll use for your order.

Figure 6.7 The account login screen.

▶ After creating an account and logging in using your e-mail address and account password, you'll get a final listing of the tracks you're about to purchase (see **Figure 6.8**). You can enter information for a credit card to use for this purchase if you don't want to use the one that is already associated with your account. To finalize your order and continue to the downloading page, click Buy Now. ❶

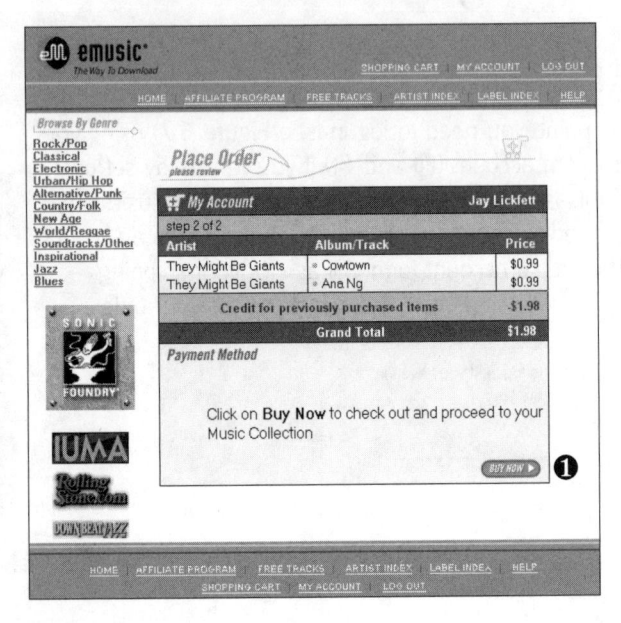

Figure 6.8 The Place Order screen is your last chance to review your order before charging your credit card.

▶ The download page (see **Figure 6.9**) is the last step! To download the tracks you've just purchased, right-click the individual links and select "save link/target as" ❶. If you are using a Mac, you will have to press CTRL while you click the link with your mouse. If you use FreeAmp, RealJukebox , or another player that supports multi-track downloads, you can download all of the tracks at once by simply clicking the Album name ❷. EMusic.com will allow three downloads of each track (with no time limit). If you're unable to download a track in three attempts, you can e-mail customer support for help.

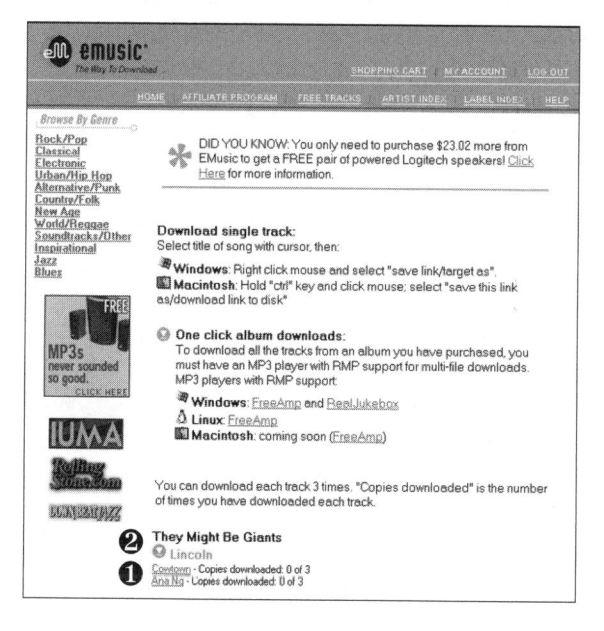

Figure 6.9 The download page provides links to the tracks you've just purchased.

Q44 If I buy MP3s online, how do I prove I actually paid for them?

Don't worry—in any legitimate MP3 transaction, you get a receipt to show you actually bought the MP3 legally.

If you're buying your MP3 tracks on a DAM CD, you'll get an invoice for your order, as well as having an actual CD with the MP3 and audio tracks on it.

If you are buying an MP3 track from EMusic.com, you don't receive physical proof of your purchase, but you do receive an e-mail receipt detailing what you bought (see **Figure 6.10**). You can also review a list of all the tracks and albums you've purchased using your account at EMusic by using the My Account portion of the Web site (see **Question 45** for more on this).

```
Order #[200041]
File Edit View Tools Message Help

From:    emusic_orders@martin.emusic.com
Date:    Friday, December 17, 1999 2:31 PM
To:      jay.lickfett@mail.com
Subject: Order #[200041]

Invoice # 0200041
Jay Lickfett
##  Description                              Price   Shipping
=============================================================
 1. Never Say Never Again (download)        $ 0.99  $ 0.00
 2. From Russia With Love (download)        $ 0.99  $ 0.00
 3. Thunderball (download)                  $ 0.99  $ 0.00
 4. Live And Let Die (download)             $ 0.99  $ 0.00
 5. Diamonds Are Forever (download)         $ 0.99  $ 0.00
                                            ================
Sub-Total                                           $ 4.95

Credit: EMusic.com Gift Certificate EM-W1R7ZXII3P   $-4.95

Grand Total                                         $ 0.00


Credits Remaining After This Purchase
EMusic.com Gift Certificate EM-W1R7ZXII3P           $ 0.05

Thanks for shopping with Emusic.com!
Any downloadable music you purchased may be accessed at:
https://secure.emusic.com/perl/secure/downloadables.pl
```

Figure 6.10 A sample e-mail receipt from EMusic.com.

Q45 What happens if my computer crashes and I lose my music?

It's good to have a certain sense of concern about losing your files if your computer should fail for some reason. While failures don't occur often, they can be devastating if you lose important documents or collections of files you've spent lots of time accumulating. For this reason, it's important to make regular backups of your data.

> **TIP**
> You can find links to several articles on how to develop a personal backup strategy and learn about the various types of media (like CD-R, tape, and Zip disk) that are often used for backups at the About.com Backup and Recovery site: **pcsupport.about.com/compute/pcsupport/msub1.htm**.

While not intended to replace a backup strategy, most sites that sell music tracks will allow you to come back in the future and re-download the ones you've purchased. For example, you can see all of your previous EMusic.com purchases in the My Account section of the site (see **Figure 6.11**). EMusic.com allows you to download each track up to three times. (If you have a legitimate need to download a track more than three times, you'll have to contact their customer service.) Having an option to go back and re-download your tracks is pretty nice—after all, you'd never be able to walk into a record store and ask for a free replacement copy of a CD you lost!

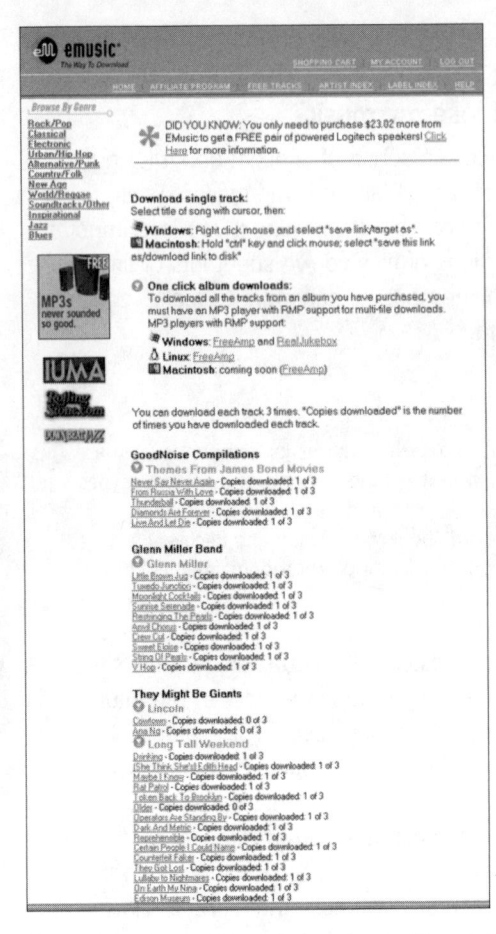

Figure 6.11 You can see a listing of everything you've ever bought at EMusic.com and download the tracks again if necessary.

Section 3
Listening to MP3 Music

7
Setting Up to Listen

Are you ready to crank up some MP3 tunes? This chapter will answer questions on what you'll need to listen to MP3s on your computer, including a review of the best MP3 software. You'll learn how to play MP3s, create playlists, and control the volume, as well as how to use more advanced features like skins and plug-ins. Let the music begin!

Q46 What do I need to listen to MP3 files on my computer?

In order to listen to MP3s, you need the following:

▶ **Pentium, Power Mac, or faster computer**—Practically speaking, you need at least a Pentium or Power Mac computer to listen to MP3 music. It might be possible to listen to MP3s on some older systems, but skipping may occur. The faster your computer's processor is, and the more memory it has, the less likely you'll have problems with your music playback—especially if you want to do other things (like surf the Web or do word processing) while listening.

▶ **Sound card (or integrated sound capability)**—The sound card in your computer is the component that converts the digital audio signal back to the analog signal that is used by typical stereo equipment, amplified computer speakers, and headphones. Most people are satisfied with the sound quality provided by their computer system, but several manufacturers produce replacement sound cards for PCs that have better sound quality (since Macs have built-in sound capability rather than a replaceable sound card, they usually aren't upgraded in this way). If you are looking for a better sound card at a reasonable price, the Creative Labs (**www.creativelabs.com**) Soundblaster Live is a popular choice, as are cards from Turtle Beach (**www.turtlebeach.com**) and Gadget Labs (**www.gadgetlabs.com**).

Computer Web sites like CNET (**www.cnet.com**) and ZD Net (**www.zdnet.com**) regularly review sound cards and are a good resource to help you find the perfect sound card upgrade.

▶ **Amplified computer speakers or headphones**—Several manufacturers make nice computer speaker systems that include a subwoofer and two satellite speakers for $100 or less, though the free speakers that often come with computer systems will also work just fine. Rather than using computer speakers, some people choose to connect the audio line out jack of their computer to an input on their stereo system for even better sound. (The cables needed to do this can be found at Radio Shack or other electronics stores.) If you're trying not to disturb others around you, headphones will also work.

▶ **MP3 playing software**—There are a number of MP3 software packages available that are quite good. The best programs include graphic equalizers (to adjust different bass and treble frequency ranges to your taste) and playlist editors, and they play a variety of digital audio formats in addition to MP3.

Some MP3 software concentrates on the playing aspect, whereas other programs include everything you need for creating, organizing, and playing MP3 files. Nearly all MP3 players are either *shareware* or *freeware*, so you can easily try several to find the one or ones you like best. We'll take a look at the leading programs in the next question.

> **TIP**
> Shareware is software that is distributed freely for a trial period. After the period has ended, however, you are obligated to pay a registration fee to the creator of the software if you intend to continue using it. Shareware is a great concept because it allows users to decide if they like a program before they pay for it. The registration fee is usually very reasonable.
>
> Freeware is software that can be downloaded and used freely with no registration fee at all, but technical support is usually not available.

Q47 What are some of the best software MP3 players?

Today, there are a number of excellent MP3 players, which range from programs dedicated to playing MP3s to programs that create and manage your MP3 collection in addition to playing it back. Some programs also give you extensive control over the look of the player using a feature known as *skins*, and some players can have new features created for them through the use of *plug-ins*.

> **TIP**
> A skin is a file that contains new graphics that can be used to change the appearance of a program. Many MP3 players allow the use of skins so that you can choose the look you like the best. The creators of MP3 player software often encourage users to create their own skins by providing information on how to do it for their program.

> **TIP**
> A plug-in is a file that can be used to add functionality to an existing program. Plug-ins often add special sound effects, or add a graphics show to go along with the music that is being played. Creators of MP3 players that support plug-ins usually encourage their users who've created new plug-ins to share them with others by submitting them to the software program's Web site.

Tables 7.1 and **7.2** list some of the most popular players for Windows and Mac. We'll cover them in more depth over the next two questions.

Table 7.1—Popular MP3Playing Software for Windows

Player	Web site	Plug-ins	Skins	MP3 Management Tools
Winamp	www.winamp.com	Y	Y	N
Sonique	www.sonique.com	Y	Y	N
MusicMatch Jukebox	www.musicmatch.com	Y	Y	Y
RealJukebox	www.realjukebox.com	Y	Y	Y

Table 7.2—Popular MP3Playing Software for Mac

Player	Web site	Plug-ins	Skins	MP3 Management Tools
MACAST	www.macast.com	Y	Y	N
SoundJam MP	www.soundjam.com	Y	Y	Y

The program you choose depends a lot on your personal taste in the interface and the way the program works. And there's nothing that says you can't use more than one program. The best way to find out what you like is to download a few and try them out.

http://www.muskalipman.com

Q48 What are the best players for Windows?

Winamp (www.winamp.com)

Winamp is one of the most popular and powerful of the digital audio players available today. Winamp is a freeware and is definitely worth the download. It plays a number of digital audio formats—including MP3, streaming MP3, and Windows Media Audio (WMA)—and it can play CDs. In addition, Liquid Audio support is promised soon. For more information on alternative digital audio formats like Windows Media Audio and Liquid Audio, refer to **Question 91**.

The Winamp player uses separate windows for the basic player interface, a graphic equalizer, and the playlist display (see **Figure 7.1**). The Winamp minibrowser is another separate window that displays information on artists from RollingStone.com and CD ordering information from Amazon.com as you listen to MP3 tracks. The windows can be open or closed in any combination, and the main player window can also be run in Windowshade mode to minimize the amount of space it takes up on your screen.

Figure 7.1 The Winamp player, equalizer, and playlist windows.

Setting up to Listen - Chapter 7

One of thousands of Winamp skins can be used to give your Winamp player a special look and feel and can be downloaded from the large collection at the Winamp Web site. Several examples are shown in **Figure 7.2**. It's also possible to create your own Winamp skin and submit it to the collection.

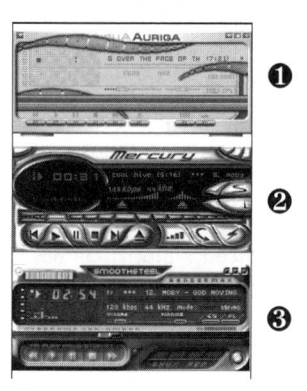

❶ Auriga skin by Andreas Lindahl
❷ Mercury skin by Mark Buchinger
❸ Smooth Steel by Marc Adell

Figure 7.2 Just some of the thousands of skins available that you can use to customize Winamp's appearance.

Winamp also allows the use of plug-ins to provide both visual and sound effects. Visualization plug-ins can be used to add a graphics effects show that is synchronized to your music. Although the visualization plug-ins are a lot of fun, the audio plug-ins can be even more useful. There are plug-ins to crossfade between tracks, equalize the volume of tracks from different albums, control tempo, and remove vocals, just to name a few.

> **TIP**
> Audio plug-ins are sometimes referred to as digital signal processing, or DSP plug-ins, because they work by altering the digital audio signal.

Sonique (www.sonique.com)

Sonique is another popular freeware player. It supports a variety of digital audio formats including MP3, streaming MP3, and WMA—and it can play audio CDs.

The Sonique player's unconventional interface can be confusing at first, but it is enjoyable to use after you get the hang of it. The player can be toggled through three different modes. Visual Mode provides access to the navigation console, the full-featured playlist editor, equalizer, and other audio settings, player configuration menus, and Web search tools. Mid-State Mode, which is shown in **Figure 7.3**, includes most of the functionality of Visual Mode in a smaller sized window. Small-State Mode takes up the least space of all.

A number of skins and visualization plug-ins are available for Sonique at the player's Web site.

> **TIP**
> Unfortunately, skins only work with the one player that they're designed for. So, you won't be able to use the Winamp skins you've downloaded with Sonique, and vice versa.

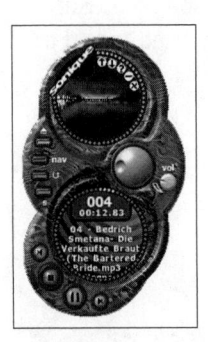

Figure 7.3 The Sonique Player in Mid-State Mode.

MusicMatch Jukebox (www.musicmatch.com)

MusicMatch Jukebox is a complete solution for creating, managing, and playing your MP3s. A free version of the software is available, as well as an enhanced version that offers faster CD ripping and encoding along with several other features for about $30. MusicMatch also plays streaming MP3, WMA, and music CDs. The program has several looks (MusicMatch calls them themes rather than skins), but it doesn't support plug-ins for visualization or sound effects. One plug-in that is available lets you download music to a Diamond Multimedia Rio portable MP3 player.

The MusicMatch music library organizes your MP3 collection and lets you sort and view your collection by artist, album, genre, and other attributes. The program allows you to create and save *playlists*, or you can use the AutoDJ feature to build a playlist according to your criteria, like genre, tempo, or mood.

MusicMatch Jukebox is a great choice if you want one program that can play and organize your music collection in an easy-to-use interface (see **Figure 7.4**).

Figure 7.4 The MusicMatch Jukebox MP3 player and music library windows.

RealJukebox (www.real.com/jukebox)

RealJukebox is another program that offers an integrated solution for encoding, managing, and playing digital audio files. Like MusicMatch Jukebox, RealJukebox comes in a free version and a Plus version that costs $30. You must buy the Plus version if you want to use the equalizer and encode MP3s at greater than 96kbps. RealJukebox can play RealAudio, Liquid Audio, and music CDs in addition to MP3. A number of RealJukebox skins are available to customize the look of the interface. Direct downloading is supported for several types of portable MP3 players, including the Diamond Multimedia Rio PMP 300 and 500, RCA Lyra, and Creative Labs' NOMAD.

The RealJukebox, shown in **Figure 7.5,** organizes your music and playlists in a Windows Explorer-like folder system, which is easy to navigate, but it doesn't offer as many ways of sorting as the MusicMatch Jukebox.

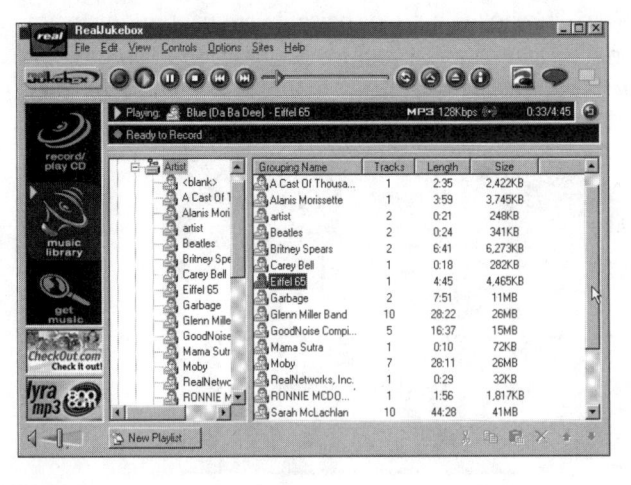

Figure 7.5 The RealJukebox MP3 player and music library.

Q49 What are the best players for Mac?

MACAST (www.macast.com)

MACAST is a good digital audio player for the Macintosh platform, capable of playing MP3, streaming MP3, and music CDs (see **Figure 7.6**). MACAST was previously known as MacAMP. A free demo version can be downloaded from the Web site, and the full version costs $25. MACAST includes an equalizer, playlist editor, and skins and supports both audio and visualization plug-ins.

Figure 7.6 MACAST's interface is clean and simple.

SoundJam MP (www.soundjam.com)

SoundJam MP is an all-in-one solution for creating and playing MP3s on a Mac (see **Figure 7.7**). It also can play streaming MP3, QuickTime, and music CDs. It supports skins and plug-ins for audio and visualization effects and has an equalizer and a playlist editor. SoundJam MP can be used to download your music to a Diamond Multimedia Rio portable player. A free, limited trial edition of SoundJam MP is available, and the full version sells for about $40.

Figure 7.7 The SoundJam MP player.

Q50 How do I play an MP3 file?

Now that you've downloaded and installed MP3 software on your computer, you're probably itching to listen to something! Because there is not room here to print the details for how to use every MP3 player, we'll just take a look at how Winamp works (see **Figure 7.8**). Although other players might look different, they all work pretty much the same way.

There are a lot of ways to queue up an MP3 track in Winamp. One way is to simply double-click the MP3 file in Windows Explorer. This opens up the Winamp player, if it isn't already open, and begins playing the track. Of course, if you installed some other program, it opens that instead of Winamp. Or, if you've installed more than one MP3 player, it might be hard to predict which program will open; this can be controlled using file associations.

TIP

Windows uses file associations to determine the default program to use for files of different types. As you install several MP3 players on your computer, they may each in turn try to take over the file associations (such as .WAV, .MP3, and .MID) for the various types of music files they play. Windows provides a tool to manage file associations (see Windows help for more on how to use it), but it's hidden away and hard to use. It's often easier to set the types of files you want each program to play from within the programs themselves.

The file association controls for several Windows MP3 players are found in the following locations:

Winamp

Open Preferences (Ctrl-P) and select Setup-File Types. The highlighted extensions are all to be associated with Winamp as their default player. If you select the "register types at Winamp start" checkbox, then Winamp will set the choices you specify each time you restart the program (in case some other program has taken over the same extensions).

Sonique

From the navigation console, choose Setup Options-File Types. Select the checkboxes for each audio file type you want Sonique to be the default player for.

MusicMatch JukeBox

From the Options menu, choose Settings. Checkboxes to select the file types to associate with MusicMatch can be found on the General tab.

RealJukebox

Under the Options menu, pick Preferences. The Update tab has the settings for music file types associated with RealJukebox as the default player.

114 Setting up to Listen - Chapter 7

Another way to queue up a track is to drag and drop the MP3 file from Windows Explorer right onto the Winamp player. Drag-and-drop can be particularly handy for queuing up more than one song at once (see **Question 52**).

Most MP3 players also have a File > Open menu command, although the command is not always easy to find in MP3 players. In Winamp, you get to the right menu by right-clicking on the top bar of the player. You can also open a file by clicking the Eject button on the front of the player.

After you have a track opened up in Winamp, you can use the play, pause, and stop controls to control the player. The forward and back arrows don't do anything unless you have several tracks queued up in a playlist.

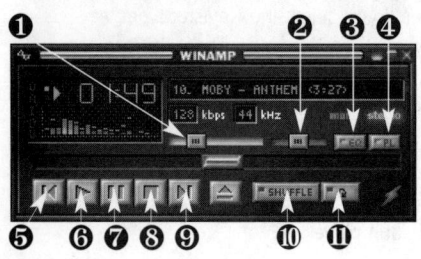

❶ Volume
❷ Balance
❸ View Equalizer
❹ View Playlist
❺ Previous Track
❻ Play
❼ Pause
❽ Stop
❾ Next Track
❿ Play Tracks in Shuffled Order
⓫ Loop Playlist

Figure 7.8 Winamp player controls.

http://www.muskalipman.com

Q51 How do I control the volume?

MP3 player software often has a volume control built right in, but this is usually only part of the picture as far as controlling volume goes. Windows has a Volume Control program that controls several aspects of the audio passing through the sound card (see **Figure 7.9**).

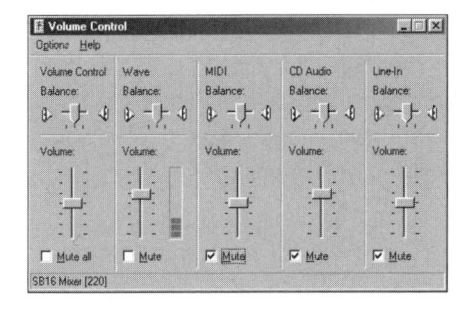

Figure 7.9 Windows Volume Control.

The Volume Control program is usually found under Programs > Accessories > Entertainment from the Start menu, or you can double-click on the small speaker icon if it shows up in the system tray. The Wave Balance control is usually the setting controlled by the MP3 player's volume setting, whereas a master control sets the overall level to the soundcard.

Another place volume can be controlled is at the amplified computer speakers, or stereo amplifier if you've hooked your stereo system up to your soundcard's line out jack. Distortion can usually be minimized by setting the volume fairly low at the speakers or amplifier and then using the Windows Volume Control program to get the desired volume. After you pick a master volume setting, you can easily control the Wave Balance volume right from the control in your MP3 player.

http://www.muskalipman.com

Q52 How do I create music playlists?

Playlists can be used to easily queue up a number of songs to be played in order. Because playlists can be saved and reused, it's possible to set up a series of songs in advance to match a particular mood or for special events. For example, you could set up separate playlists of music for a quiet, romantic dinner, music to work out with or a long playlist of music for a party with your friends. MusicMatch Jukebox includes an AutoDJ feature that builds playlists for you based on criteria you give it and the information stored in the ID3 tags of each track. Many players also have a randomizer that lets you mix up the tracks in a playlist for a little variety.

Playlists take up very little storage space, because they have just enough information to tell the player where to find the actual MP3 files. However, this means that if you rearrange your MP3 files on your computer's hard drive, your playlists won't know where to find them.

Let's use Winamp, shown in **Figure 7.10**, as our example of a playlist editor. Most other players' editors are similar.

Just as there are several ways of playing a single MP3 track, there is more than one way to select songs to go into a playlist. One of the easiest ways is to drag and drop individual MP3 files or entire folders of files onto the playlist from Windows Explorer. Alternatively, you can use the Add File or Add Folder commands of the playlist. On Winamp, these are located under the ADD button at the bottom of the playlist window. Other buttons let you remove songs, reorder the songs in several ways, and save or load playlists. Songs can be rearranged within a playlist by dragging them to a new position. You can also double-click a song in the playlist to begin playing it immediately.

Figure 7.10 Clicking the ADD button reveals Add File, Add Directory, and Add URL buttons.

Q53. How can I use skins?

Skins are a fun way to personalize your player (refer back to **Figure 7.2** for a few example skins). Skins are also easy to install. Here are the steps to change Winamp skins:

▶ Browse the skins listing at the Winamp Web site (www.winamp.com) to find a cool skin you like.

▶ Left-click the Download link for the skin you want to try. The skin downloads and installs itself automatically.

It's that easy! Other programs require slightly different steps, so check your player's documentation for directions.

To switch between skins in Winamp, press Alt-S. This will show you a list of the skins you've downloaded and installed. Now just click on the name of the skin you want to set as the current look of your player.

Q54 How can I use plug-ins?

Winamp has also made plug-ins very easy to install with its plug-in installation utility, known tongue-in-cheek as the Nullsoft PIMP Installer. Before this utility was available, plug-in files had to be copied manually into one or more Winamp and system folders. Some older plug-ins might not use the installer utility, and you'll have to follow the instructions that are provided with the plug-in to install it.

To install and configure a Winamp plug-in that uses the installer utility, follow these steps:

1. Browse the collection of plug-ins found at the Winamp Web site (**www.winamp.com**).

2. Right-click on the Download link for the plug-in you've chosen. Choose Save This Program to Disk and specify a location on your hard drive to save the plug-in files.

3. After the plug-in file has been downloaded, double-click it to begin the installation and follow the instructions that are provided.

4. To configure and start the plug-in in Winamp, right-click the top of the player window and select Options > Preferences. The Preferences window, which is shown in **Figure 7.11**, is where all plug-ins are controlled. (Ctrl-P is a quick shortcut to open this window).

5. Find the plug-in that you installed in the listings.

6. Select the plug-in by single-clicking it in the right half of the Preferences window. Some plug-ins, but not all, have Start, Stop, and Configure buttons. These buttons can be used to control the plug-in.

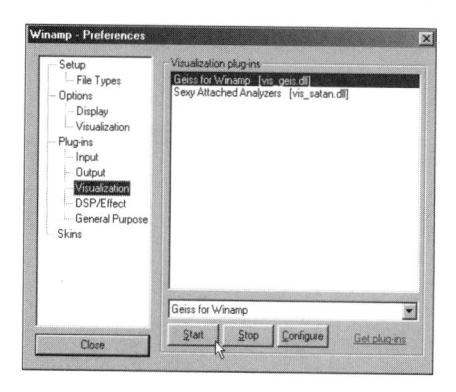

Figure 7.11 Getting ready to start a visualization plug-in in the Winamp Preferences window.

> **TIP**
>
> The Output plug-in selection determines where the decoded audio signal created by Winamp ends up. For normal playback it should be set to use the Nullsoft WaveOut plug-in. If Winamp mysteriously stops playing after you've been working with plug-in settings, make sure you didn't accidentally change the Output plug-in to something other than WaveOut. The Nullsoft Disk Writer output plug-in is another one that is commonly used—it converts MP3 tracks into WAV files and saves them on your hard drive instead of playing them though your speakers.

> **TIP**
>
> Plug-ins, especially visualization ones, can use up a lot of your computer's processing power. So, if you have an older computer, you may not be able to enjoy the latest and greatest plug-ins. If your MP3s seem to be skipping when you play them, try disabling any visualization or audio plug-ins you're using to see if that eliminates the problem.

http://www.muskalipman.com

8

Net Radio—Streaming MP3

Q55 What are Net radio stations and streaming audio?

Streaming is a method of transferring multimedia, such as audio or video, in one continuous feed from a sender to a receiver. A streaming server parcels out a little at a time to everyone who is connected to it, and those receiving the stream can play it as it arrives without having to wait for a whole file to download. You can think of an audio stream as being similar to a radio broadcast, whereas downloading an entire audio file before you're able to listen to it is more like buying a cassette. The ability to begin hearing the audio or viewing the video without first having to download the entire file makes streaming particularly useful for multimedia, which tends to require large files even when it's compressed using MP3 or other methods.

Streaming is often used as a way to sample a song and decide if you really want to spend the time downloading the entire file. Many Web-based music sites provide a link you can click on to hear a streaming audio clip. Sometimes, as in the case of MP3.com's site, the entire song is available in a stream. In most cases, however, the sample is only a portion of the song. For example, CDnow.com offers 30-second streaming clips of tracks in the RealAudio format (another type of digital audio format that is popular for streaming audio—see **Question 57** for more).

Streaming is also particularly useful for longer, continuous Web broadcasts similar to conventional television and radio broadcasting. In fact, thousands of continuously streaming audio servers known as *Net radio* stations have sprung up on the Web. Some of these stations are run by traditional media outlets, such as radio stations rebroadcasting their normal programs. Others are run by companies that generate revenue with advertising (ads interspersed in the programming or banner ads displayed while the user listens) or by selling CDs of the music played on their stations. A large proportion of Net radio stations are run by people who simply enjoy having the power to be the DJ or who want to choose the songs they play on their own radio station. Just as the MP3 movement is shifting power away from the big record companies to the independent artists and consumers, streaming audio technology makes it possible for almost anyone to create and run his own radio station, giving consumers much more choice over what they listen to.

> **NOTE**
> A Web broadcast using streaming technology is often called *Webcasting*.

Q56 Why is Net radio so popular?

One of the advantages of Net radio is that there are thousands of stations providing more variety and control over what you want to hear. Many stations follow a theme (such as, all '60s rock and roll, sci-fi movie themes, or classical piano), whereas others play a broader mix of music. Vast numbers of Net radio stations can exist and can cater to very narrow niches because they are easy and inexpensive to run, opening up the field to almost anyone who wants to be a Webcaster. Additionally, the Digital Millennium Copyright Act of 1998 has made it easier to get permission to play copyrighted music owned by the record companies, which means that it's possible to find both mainstream and independent music being played by Net radio stations.

Unlike conventional broadcast radio, Net radio reaches a global audience as easily as it reaches a local audience. This opens up the world to the listener, and you will find many international stations Webcasting local music or other content you might otherwise never experience. Or you could enjoy your hometown local news although you are on the other side of the country.

Another nice feature of Net radio is that almost all stations display the names of the song and artist currently playing. (How many times have you tried unsuccessfully to figure out what song a regular radio station is playing?) Many stations link to information on the artist or even to a site where you can purchase the CD or download more tracks.

Net radio station listeners usually don't have to put up with listening to annoying ads every couple of songs. Most noncommercial Net radio stations run by individuals don't have any ads at all, and those that do tend to keep them to a minimum. Commercial stations, most of which still rely on ads, sometimes use banner ads, which are much less obtrusive than cutting into the programming. In the future, some commercial Net radio stations could forgo all ads and rely on subscriptions or very small pay-per-listen fees to support themselves.

Q57 What are the major streaming audio formats?

Streaming audio is often provided using the MP3 format. Nullsoft, the maker of the Winamp player, calls its popular streaming MP3 server *SHOUTcast*. As a result, streaming MP3 is sometimes referred to as SHOUTcasting. Winamp and most other popular MP3 players can handle streaming MP3.

The other major streaming audio formats are RealNetworks' RealAudio and Microsoft's *Windows Media*. These formats typically require separate player software. Both of these formats provide protection schemes to prevent unauthorized copying, which makes them more popular than MP3 with some audio providers who want to retain close control over their content. However, there is always someone who can figure out a way to get around these copy protection schemes (as seen in **Question 58**). It remains to be seen whether RealAudio or Windows Media will come out on top, and while these two proprietary formats battle, streaming MP3 remains very popular because of its widespread support in digital audio player software.

Q58 What are the disadvantages of streaming audio versus downloading audio?

Although you can listen to an audio stream almost immediately after your software connects to the server providing it, streaming audio does have some disadvantages.

One disadvantage is that your network connection must be fast enough to receive the audio signal in roughly real time, where you're not constrained to any particular time limit with a file download. For most listeners, this currently means that, to be received smoothly, streaming audio must be lower quality than downloaded audio. Software used to listen to a stream tries to keep ahead of itself by pre-buffering audio, much like a portable CD player buffers music to prevent skips or breaks in the music when the player is jostled. Buffering the audio stream of Net radio can help prevent skips due to occasional bursts of heavy network traffic, but buffering can work only so far ahead. Net radio stations broadcast at bitrates ranging from AM radio quality to near CD quality, and you have to experiment to find what bitrates work well with your Internet connection type. As high-speed Internet access becomes more widespread, this quality issue will disappear, as it will be possible to get just as high a quality in real time as when downloading a file.

Perhaps streaming audio's biggest disadvantage is that you have to be connected to the Internet in order to listen. This is less of a problem for listeners with cable modems or DSL, which can be connected all the time without accumulating hourly charges or tying up a phone line. Listeners who rely on modems to dial up may find it a little less convenient, although several products that can record streaming audio to be played back later (without requiring a network connection) may help.

Until recently, streaming audio wasn't easy to save for playback. This is beginning to change with the introduction of software such as StreamboxVCR (**www.streambox.com**) and Voquette Media Manager (**www.voquette.com**). The Voquette Media Manager can be used to save streaming audio through the audio out jack of your soundcard to a cassette tape recorder or a MiniDisc recorder for playback. Voquette is testing software that also allows saving the audio to a Rio player. The StreamboxVCR software is similar, but it records directly to the computer's hard drive, where the audio can be easily saved and played back any time or downloaded to a portable digital audio player.

RealNetworks filed a lawsuit against Streambox in December 1999, alleging that StreamboxVCR violates copyright law in bypassing RealAudio's copy protection scheme. In January 2000, the court granted an injunction preventing the further distribution of the StreamboxVCR software until the case is resolved. A final decision against Streambox would be a blow to consumers who want to use time-shifting and space-shifting tools in a legitimate fashion, so this case will be closely watched in the digital audio world.

Q59 Where can I find Net radio stations?

Listening to a Net radio station is easy. Usually, you just click on a link on a Web page, and your player software starts right up. The trickiest part is actually finding the stations. After all, there is no Scan button like the one on your radio receiver! Some great places to start finding Net radio stations are listed here. In addition to these sites, check out other MP3 portal Web sites, such as MP3.com and RollingStone.com, which often offer Net radio in addition to downloadable files.

MP3 Net Radio

Live365.com (www.live365.com)

Live365.com (see **Figure 8.1**) offers a free streaming MP3 broadcasting service to anyone who wants to sign up to run his own Net radio station, and all of the stations listed on this site are actually streaming from Live365.com's own servers. Live365.com has obtained the appropriate licenses for Net broadcasting under the provisions of the Digital Millennium Copyright Act, so that people who create their own stations using the Live365.com service can broadcast just about any music they legally obtain without having to worry about doing their own licensing.

As a result, the site is an excellent place to find thousands of reliable Net radio stations playing a wide selection of music. You can browse by genre and description to find a station you like, and you can limit the stations displayed to only those you can tune in to with your Internet connection speed. Listeners rate stations, which can also help you find the best ones to try.

To listen to Live365.com stations, you need only your Web browser and a streaming MP3 player. Live365.com suggests using RealPlayer 7, Winamp, Sonique, or MusicMatch for Windows users; or Audion, MACAST, or SoundJam MP for Mac users. When you're playing a station, a small browser window displays the last three songs played.

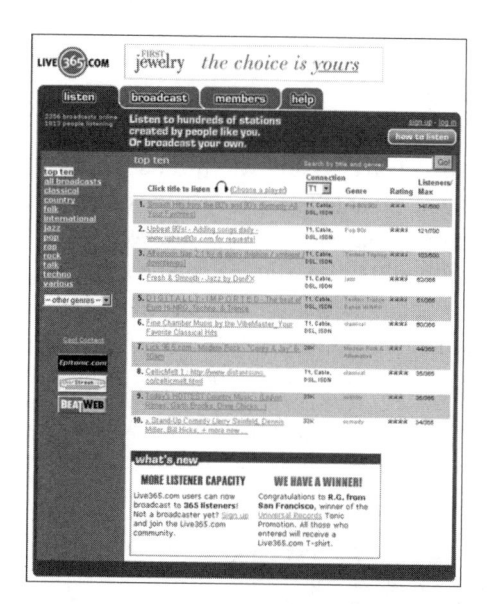

Figure 8.1 Live365.com lists thousands of Net radio stations.

SHOUTcast Showcase (www.shoutcast.com)

Check out the SHOUTcast Showcase to see a listing of streaming MP3 Net radio stations run by people using SHOUTcast software. The directory displays stations run by individuals on their own servers as well as those run by centralized services like Live365.com. The listings are organized by genre for browsing. Many stations display the current song that is playing.

Nullsoft recommends using the latest version of its Winamp for listening, but other players that support streaming MP3 should also work fine.

iCAST (www.icast.com)

This media portal includes a number of MP3 Net radio stations, which they call iCAST Streams. To listen, you can download their free iCASTER media player, which includes instant messaging to let you chat with your friends in addition to playing MP3s and several other audio formats. Other players that support streaming MP3s also work fine for listening to iCAST streams.

http://www.muskalipman.com

Non-MP3 Net Radio

Spinner.com (www.spinner.com)

On AOL's Spinner.com, (see **Figure 8.2**) you can listen to one of more than 120 RealAudio stations, each of which concentrates on a specific genre of music. Spinner lets you save your favorite stations as presets and offers artist information and news. Links are provided to purchase the CD containing the song currently playing, and you can even add the current song information to a list Spinner calls the Soundpad. This way, you can keep track of songs you like and want to learn more about or purchase later.

To listen to the Spinner.com stations, you need a RealAudio player and the Spinner.com player, which can be downloaded for free from the Web site.

Figure 8.2 Listening to a Spinner.com station using the Spinner Plus player.

Yahoo! broadcast (www.broadcast.com)

Yahoo! broadcast (formerly known simply as Broadcast.com) is one of the leaders in Net radio and offers one of the widest arrays of stations and archived programs. The choices include continuous broadcasts of hundreds of traditional radio stations and live broadcasts of events like college and professional sports, concerts, and other special events. Many of these broadcasts are archived, so you can listen to them even if you missed the live broadcast. Yahoo! broadcast streams audio in Windows Media and RealAudio formats.

Yesterday USA (www.yesterdayusa.com)

At this site, you will find a RealAudio stream of Yesterday USA Radio, which rebroadcasts vintage radio programs and music from the 1920s through 1950s, as well as programs on the history of radio broadcasting. The service is supported by listener donations and is associated with the nonprofit National Museum of Communications. The Web site includes a schedule of its programming for two-week periods.

NetRadio.com (www.netradio.com)

This site features a Net radio station playing music from mainstream artists for each of 120 genres and categories of music! As you listen to a station, a browser window displays the current song and a link where you can order the CD from the CDPoint online music store. The stations also air ads for their CDs and current specials.

The NetRadio stations' streams are available in either Windows Media or RealAudio format and require at least a 56k modem connection.

DiscJockey.com (www.discjockey.com)

DiscJockey.com is another good site with a large selection of stations offered in Windows Media and RealAudio formats. Listeners can rate songs and send in requests and dedications through the Web interface of the station they're listening to. The dedication messages are displayed along with the title and performer of the song being played.

9

MP3 on the Go—Portable Players

Q60 Is there a convenient way to listen to MP3 when I'm on the go?

When the MP3 movement was just getting started, the only way to listen was by using MP3 player software on a personal computer. A laptop computer could be used as a somewhat portable MP3 player, but it was bulky, inconvenient, and expensive. Some dedicated hobbyists installed computers into their cars to create a mobile MP3 system, but these were custom built, required the user to wire the computer into the car's electrical system, and were generally difficult to use.

Luckily for MP3 lovers, a number of mass-produced, handheld MP3 players are now available, as well as players designed to be mounted into a car. Although portable players still require a computer to store music until it's downloaded to the player, they allow you to take your MP3s just about anywhere. Most players today hold about an album's worth of music at a time, and some have the capability to store hundreds or even thousands of songs. We'll take a look at and compare several of the players that are available today later in **Question 65**.

Q61 I already have a portable CD player, so why would I want a portable MP3 player, too?

Portable MP3 players have several advantages over regular personal CD players. For one thing, MP3 players can be made to fit into very small, lightweight packages. Many players are similar in size to a deck of playing cards. MP3 players also don't skip when jostled, and there are no moving parts to break or wear out.

A portable MP3 player can also be better than a CD player if you find that you enjoy downloading tracks from the Web. Although you could burn your own music CDs from your downloaded MP3 files, it's much more convenient to simply transfer the files directly to a player.

Some new MP3 players include a normal CD player in addition to the capability to play MP3 files. This type of device might be just what you're looking for if you want the convenience of the MP3 player but don't want to give up the ability to also play music CDs using the same device.

There are some disadvantages to MP3 players, although many people feel they are easily outweighed by the advantages. At around $200, portable MP3 players still cost more than personal CD players. Also, with most players, you have to transfer music from your computer to the player each time you want to listen to a different album. This is not true of some of the new players that can play MP3 files stored on a CD, because the disc can be swapped just as easily as a music CD. The download problem is also addressed by high-capacity portable players, because you aren't as likely to need to download a new album if you already have a substantial portion of your music collection (or all of it!) already with you.

Q62. How do I get music from my computer to my portable player?

In order to transfer MP3s from your computer to a portable player, you'll first need to connect the two with a cable. Some players use a docking station that is connected to the computer rather than a cable directly between the player and the computer (see **Figure 9.1**). You then use the software that came with the player to move the files. You may also be able to choose an MP3 playing program for your computer that supports downloads to your portable player. For example, MusicMatch can be used with several portables, including the Diamond Rio and Creative Labs Nomad.

❶ Nomad player
❷ Docking station

Figure 9.1 The Creative NOMAD player connects to a computer through its docking station.

Current portable MP3 players use one of the following two types of cables for transferring files from a computer:

▶ **Parallel Port**—Many portable MP3 players connect to a PC's *parallel port*, which is also commonly used for printers and scanners. Nearly all IBM-compatible PCs have parallel ports, but Macintosh computers do not.

▶ **Universal Serial Bus (USB)**—Quite a few of the newer portable MP3 players connect to the source computer via USB. Most PCs and Macintosh computers have a *USB* interface. Using a USB connection is less likely to interfere with your printer and allows faster transfers between your computer and portable player.

If you're considering buying a portable MP3 player, make sure you know which of these interfaces are available on your computer. Also, check that the player comes with software that supports your operating system, or you won't be able to transfer music to your player!

Q63 How do portable MP3 players store the music?

Most portable MP3 players store music using a combination of built-in and removable memory cards. The permanent on-board memory capacity is often 32MB, which can hold about one half-hour of CD-quality music, or 64MB, corresponding to just over an hour of music. If the music has been encoded at a lower bitrate, more music can be stored in the same space, but the quality will not be as good. (The relationship between bitrate, quality, and storage space is discussed in **Chapter 1**, "MP3—The Format") In addition to the built-in memory, the portable device often has an expansion slot for one of several formats of small memory card. These memory cards allow you to carry more music to swap in and out of the player, which helps minimize the number of transfers you have to make between your computer and the player. Although these cards are still fairly expensive, prices most likely will continue to fall and capacities will rise, making it convenient to carry more of your music with you.

SmartMedia Cards

The most common type of expansion memory currently used by portable MP3 players is the *SmartMedia* card. (SmartMedia is the trademarked name for solid state floppy disk card, or SSFDC.) The size of a SmartMedia card is similar to that of a business card cut in half—a mere 45mm by 37mm by 0.76mm. Though they are small, these memory cards can hold quite a bit of information, with capacities ranging from 2MB to 64MB.

Although SmartMedia cards are generally very convenient and easy to use, there are several things to watch out for. First, not all SmartMedia cards are compatible with all MP3 players, so make sure you check the capacity limitations of your player before purchasing any new memory. Some MP3 players may not be able to recognize high-capacity SmartMedia cards introduced after the player was designed. Secondly, SmartMedia cards come in two different voltages—3.3V and 5V. You should be certain you know which of these two card voltages is needed for use with your player to avoid damaging the SmartMedia cards. Finally, while many digital cameras also use SmartMedia, it's usually recommended that you don't interchange the memory cards between a camera and an MP3 player. This is because some players (notably, the Diamond Multimedia Rio line) reformat the cards, making them unusable in a digital camera.

CompactFlash Cards

CompactFlash cards, a second type of small removable memory used in MP3 players, are approximately the same size of a book of matches (43mm by 36mm by 3.3mm). A thicker, higher-capacity version of the cards, called Type II CompactFlash, has also been defined and is 5mm thick. The capacity of current CompactFlash memory cards ranges from 8MB to 160MB.

CompactFlash cards don't typically have the maximum supported capacity or voltage compatibility issues that SmartMedia cards have. However, while the original Type I and the newer Type II cards are the same electronically speaking, make sure that your player physically can accept the thicker Type II cards if you're shopping for additional CompactFlash capacity.

http://www.muskalipman.com

Other Storage Media

Although most portable MP3 players use memory cards for storage, others are taking a different route. Several players that should be available this year actually include a small hard drive that can provide gigabytes of storage space—enough for hundreds of hours of MP3 audio. For the most part, these portable players are larger, because of the space taken up by the internal disk drive. However, IBM has developed a miniature hard drive called the microdrive, which is the same size as a Type II CompactFlash card. Future MP3 players might be able to interchange normal CompactFlash cards and microdrives, which can hold hundreds of megabytes of MP3 music.

Several other players that can read MP3 files from a compact disc are also becoming available. To use these, you must purchase MP3 files on compact disc or burn your own disks using a CD-R drive. Some of these disc-based players also include built-in or removable memory that can be used like the more common portable players. If you plan on burning CDs to store your MP3 files anyway, or if you want to listen to music CDs with the same player, a player that uses disc-based storage might be the most convenient for you.

Q64 Can I listen to MP3 in my car?

People often want to listen to their MP3 music in their car, and there are several different ways this can be accomplished. Some portable MP3 systems, such as the empeg player (**www.empeg.com**), are designed to completely replace your existing system, providing the ultimate solution in car audio. These players typically include a radio tuner and very large capacity, but they are still prohibitively expensive for most people, because they are essentially a computer system dedicated to playing digital audio. The price of these players should drop into a more reasonable range as more manufacturers start to produce them.

If you want to listen to your MP3 files through your existing audio system, you have a couple of options. If your system has a conveniently located input jack, you can simply connect a portable MP3 player to it directly, just as you would a portable CD player. A cassette tape adapter that slips into the car's tape player and plugs into the headphone jack of an audio source is also an inexpensive way of playing MP3 in your car, although the quality is not as good as plugging directly into an input jack. There's even one MP3 player—the rome (**www.romemp3.com**)—that is shaped like an audio cassette (see **Figure 9.2**). The entire player can be inserted into a car's tape player and played as if it were a normal cassette tape!

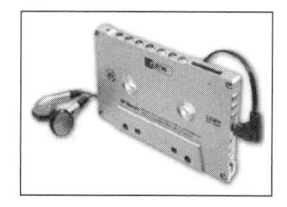

Figure 9.2 The rome functions like a normal portable MP3 player, or it can be played through a normal audio cassette player.

> **TIP**
> The MP3 Car Web site (**www.mp3car.com**) has lots of examples of hobbyists who have built their own MP3 car audio systems, as well as lots of links to information on portable players.

Q65 What are some of the best portable MP3 players?

Here are a just a few of the portable MP3 players now available. MP3 portal sites like MP3.com (www.mp3.com) often review new players and are a good place to find out more about the latest portables.

Diamond Multimedia Rio (www.riohome.com)

The Diamond Multimedia Rio PMP 300 was one of the first widely available portable MP3 players and remains very popular. It comes with 32MB of onboard memory and can be expanded to a maximum 64MB with a SmartMedia card. It uses a parallel port for music transfers and has straightforward controls and a basic display.

A new generation of the Rio player, called the Rio 500, has also been released (see **Figure 9.3**). It features transfers using USB rather than a parallel port, and software is available for both Windows and Mac OS users. The Rio 500 comes with 64MB of onboard memory that can be expanded up to 96MB using a SmartMedia card.

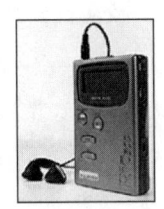

Figure 9.3 Rio 500 portable player.

Creative Labs Nomad (www.nomadworld.com)

The NOMAD portable player distinguishes itself with its recording capability (using a built-in microphone), an integrated FM radio, and stylish magnesium case. It comes with 32MB of memory and can be upgraded using a SmartMedia card.

The next-generation NOMAD II can be upgraded to support digital audio formats other than MP3, including Windows Media. It also has a larger LCD display than the original NOMAD. Instead of having onboard memory, the NOMAD II relies exclusively on its SmartMedia card for storage (a 64MB card is included). The NOMAD II uses USB but includes software only for Windows users.

The NOMAD Jukebox (see **Figure 9.4**) should store up to 6GB of MP3, Windows Media, or WAV files on an integrated hard drive. Like the NOMAD II, it can be upgraded to support additional audio formats, and it also uses a USB interface.

Figure 9.4 The NOMAD Jukebox.

TurboMP3 (www.turbomp3.com)

The TurboMP3 player (see **Figure 9.5**) has a very large, easy-to-read LCD screen and comes with 32MB of onboard memory, with an open SmartMedia slot for expansion. It also includes built-in recording capability.

Figure 9.5 The TurboMP3 portable player.

Vertical Horizon Eclectic CP-200 (www.evhi.com)

The Eclectic is an example of a disc-based portable MP3 player that can play either MP3 files from a CD or regular music CDs. It also includes an optional SmartMedia slot. This player is expected to cost only slightly more than a good portable CD player.

Section 4

Creating Your Own MP3 Files

10

Getting Ready to Rip

One of the best aspects of MP3 is that just about anyone can create his or her own MP3 files. That means you don't necessarily have to buy your music in MP3 format, because your favorite CDs, records, tapes, or audio in any other format can be converted to MP3. It also helps open up the world of home recording to nearly anyone with a PC.

This section of the book will cover what you need to do to create your own MP3s. Saving music onto your computer is the first step, and you'll learn how to do this by either ripping music from CDs or recording from another source, like your LP collection, in a process called digital audio capture. Once you've got the music recorded on your computer, you'll learn how to use an encoder, a program that converts the music to an MP3 file. In the next several chapters, you'll learn about software that makes the ripping and encoding process easy. We'll also take a look at a couple of things that help you get the most out of your MP3 collection, as well as some ideas for sharing your own music in MP3 format with others.

Getting Ready to Rip

This chapter will cover setting up the various things you'll need to make your own MP3s, including what hardware you'll need in your computer and the best programs for ripping your CDs and encoding the songs as MP3s. You'll also be introduced to the subject of digital audio capture and recording audio from sources other than a CD. By the end of this chapter, you should be ready to work with the software you choose to actually create your MP3s.

Q66 What do I need to convert my music CDs to MP3 format?

Creating MP3s from a CD collection is one of the first things people want to do when they get interested in listening to MP3s. Before you get started, you'll need to install the software required to rip the audio from a CD and encode it in the MP3 format. (Ripping is the process of reading the digital information that represents music from the CD, and encoding is the process of converting the music read from the CD into an MP3 file.) You'll also want to make sure you have the right computer hardware to get the job done. The basic checklist of things you'll need is as follows:

▶ Ripping software

▶ Encoding software

▶ Pentium or better PC (or Power Mac)

▶ Plenty of free hard drive space

▶ CD-ROM drive that supports digital audio extraction

There are quite a few programs available for ripping audio from CDs and for encoding the tracks in the MP3 format. Some programs, like AudioCatalyst and MusicMatch Jukebox, have even integrated these two operations into the same package, which is usually the most convenient way to create MP3s. Instead of having to set up the ripping and encoding steps using two separate programs, you can use one combined package to set up your ripping session, take a break, and come back to your completed MP3 files. Some of the best software for ripping and encoding is described in the next question.

NOTE
While "ripping" a CD certainly sounds somewhat painful, it won't hurt the CD in any way. A ripper simply reads the digital information stored on the disc.

Extracting audio from CDs and encoding them as MP3 files is fairly demanding on your computer's processor, and most software calls for, at minimum, a Pentium-class PC (or a Power Mac). Keep in mind that the faster your computer is, the less time it will take to create your MP3s. Similarly, hard drive space will disappear pretty quickly if you're planning on creating more than a few MP3 files. Remember that even though it's compressed, a CD-quality MP3 file takes up around 1MB of drive space per minute of audio. If the ripping software you use creates WAV files as an intermediate step in the ripping process, you need even more free hard drive space (see **Question 72** for more on this).

You'll also want a CD-ROM drive that supports digital audio extraction, or DAE (see **Question 68**). Digital audio extraction allows the ripping software to read the digital information directly from the CD. If your drive isn't able to do DAE, you may still be able to record the songs from the CD by setting your ripping software to record the audio as it is played through your sound card. This recording, or analog extraction, technically is not ripping, but many of the programs that rip CDs are capable of using this method if DAE fails. Digital extraction is preferred because it avoids hiss, pops, and clicks that can be introduced in the analog extraction method. Digital extraction is also much faster because, unlike analog extraction, it doesn't have to work in real time as the track plays.

Q67 What are some of the best programs for ripping and encoding CDs?

Most people find it most convenient to use a single program that can rip CDs as well as encode the tracks as MP3s. AudioCatalyst and MusicMatch Jukebox are two of the most popular programs of this type.

Xing AudioCatalyst (www.audiocatalyst.com)

AudioCatalyst is a popular ripper/encoder package because it is both powerful and easy to use. The AudioCatalyst interface (see **Figure 10.1**) is simple and doesn't distract you with a lot of unnecessary extras. However, AudioCatalyst includes support for all the features you could want, including CDDB support to automatically retrieve CD track information, the ability to save as a WAV file or encode directly as MP3 files, normalization to correct differences in volume across albums, and support for a number of quality levels up to 320 kbps (these features are all explained as they are used in the next chapter, "Ripping and Encoding"). A free demo version of AudioCatalyst is available for download from Xing's Web site, and the full version can be purchased there for $30.

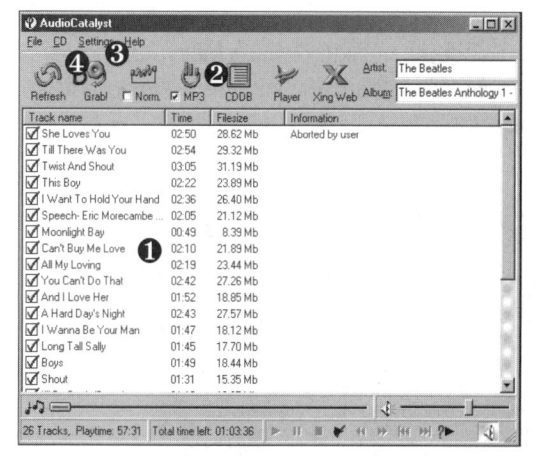

① Tracks for the current CD are listed in the main window.
② Pressing the CDDB button retrieves track and album titles automatically.
③ Configuration settings for ripping and encoding are found in the Settings Menu.
④ The Grab! button begins the ripping and encoding process.

Figure 10.1 The AudioCatalyst interface is easy to use.

MusicMatch Jukebox (www.musicmatch.com)

The MusicMatch Jukebox (see **Figure 10.2**) is another very popular package that includes the capability to rip CDs as well as encode the MP3 files. As its name implies, it also can be used to manage the MP3 files you create or download. Like AudioCatalyst, MusicMatch features ripping and encoding with the touch of a single button, along with many other features such as CDDB support, saving files in WAV, MP3, or Windows Media formats, and a choice of encoding at many quality levels. MusicMatch also has the capability to record from sources that are plugged into your sound card (see **Question 69**). Managing

MusicMatch's configuration settings may be easier for beginners than AudioCatalyst. A demo version of MusicMatch Jukebox is available at the MusicMatch Web site, and the full version can be purchased there for $30.

❶ The MusicMatch Jukebox Recorder window is used to rip CDs.
❷ Track information for the current CD is retrieved from the CDDB.
❸ Selected tracks are ripped and encoded using the Recorder controls.
❹ As tracks are encoded, they are added to the MusicMatch Jukebox Library.

Figure 10.2 MusicMatch Jukebox is an excellent program for creating MP3s.

AudioCatalyst and MusicMatch Jukebox aren't the only good programs for ripping and encoding. **Table 10.1** lists a few others that you may want to take a look at.

Table 10.1—MP3 Rippers and Encoders

Name/ Cost	Web site/ Notes
AudioCatalyst $30 (free trial)	**www.audiocatalyst.com** ripper/encoder for Windows and Mac
MusicMatch Jukebox $30 (basic version free)	**www.musicmatch.com** ripper/encoder/player for Windows
AudioActive Production Studio $270 ("lite" version $60)	**www.audioactive.com** encoder for Windows, oriented towards audio pros
RealJukebox $30 (basic version free)	**www.realjukebox.com** ripper/encoder/player for Windows
SoundJam MP $40 (free trial)	**www.soundjam.com** ripper/encoder/player for Mac
Streambox Ripper $35 (free trial)	**www.streambox.com/ Products/Ripper/index.asp** ripper/encoder for Windows, also converts RealAudio to MP3
Visiosonic PCDJ $30 (basic version free)	**www.visiosonic.com/ products/pcdjphat.htm** ripper/encoder/player for Windows

Q68 How can I tell if my CD-ROM drive supports digital audio extraction?

Fortunately, most CD-ROM drives support digital audio extraction. If you're not sure if yours does, it's probably easiest just to try using one of the ripping programs in digital extraction mode (almost always the default setting) and see if it works. If it does, great!

If your first attempts at ripping using digital audio extraction fail, there still are several things you can try. First, check the manual for your CD-ROM drive (or the manufacturer's Web site) and see if it mentions digital audio extraction compatibility. Alternatively, you can check one of several compatibility listings maintained on the Web. MP3.com maintains one such listing at **help.mp3.com/help/faqs/make-cdlist.html**.

If you still think your CD-ROM drive should be able to do digital audio extraction after checking these sources, you might have an issue with the drivers used for your CD-ROM drive. Try reading the documentation of the ripping software you're using to resolve driver issues or try using a different ripping program.

> **TIP**
> AudioCatalyst has one of the better troubleshooting sections of all the ripping software packages. If you're really stuck, try installing AudioCatalyst and follow its documentation.

Even if your CD-ROM drive doesn't support digital audio extraction, not all is lost. Most likely, you'll still be able to record tracks using the analog extraction setting of your ripping software. If you must do this, keep in mind the quality of your sound card will have an impact on the quality of your MP3s. Sound card quality is discussed in more detail in the next question.

Q69. Can I convert audio from other sources (like LP or tape) to MP3?

When creating MP3 files, you definitely aren't limited to using music CDs as a source. In fact, it's possible to capture audio from just about any source that has an audio line out jack by connecting it to the line in jack on your sound card. This digital audio capture process is basically the same as recording a CD in analog mode, because it is depending on the sound card to sample the audio source into a digital format. After the audio has been recorded on the computer in a digital format, typically a WAV file, it can be converted to an MP3 file using an encoder such as the ones discussed earlier in this chapter.

> **TIP**
>
> There are usually several connectors on a sound card, including jacks for line input, line output, and a microphone. The line out jack is used for playing sound through externally amplified speakers, whereas line in and microphone jacks are for getting audio into the computer. If you're trying to capture audio though your sound card, make sure your audio source's line out is connected to the line in jack of the sound card rather than the microphone input. You should also avoid plugging any non-line level outputs (basically anything that normally drives a speaker) into the line in jack of your sound card to avoid damaging it. The microphone input usually isn't suitable for high-quality recording, so if you're actually using a microphone, patch it through a microphone pre-amp into the line-in jack of your sound card.

http://www.muskalipman.com

The main disadvantage of capturing audio through a sound card rather than ripping directly from a CD is that the quality of your equipment, especially that of the sound card, is going to limit the quality of the end result. If you're ripping from a CD, you can be pretty sure the master recording was transferred to that CD as near to perfect as possible. By ripping the exact digital recording, you're taking advantage of the recording studio quality of the original. If you're capturing audio from some other source through your own sound card, it's unlikely you'll achieve the same result. That isn't to say you can't get good results; it just means you have to make a larger investment in equipment to get the same quality as if you were ripping directly from a CD.

Typical sound cards, such as the Sound Blaster brand cards, are probably quite adequate for most people when it comes to capturing audio for creating MP3s. However, higher-quality sound cards are available that are targeted at the audiophile market. These high-end cards offer more complex (and therefore more expensive) circuitry, which results in less background noise. Many of these cards offer additional features popular with audio enthusiasts, such as multiple inputs for mixing. If you want to capture the highest-quality audio possible from a high-quality analog source, you might want to invest in a premium sound card; otherwise, you'll probably do just fine with your existing one.

> **TIP**
> Sound cards use circuits called analog-to-digital converters (often shortened to A/D converters, or ADCs) to convert the source signal to a digital representation through the sampling process described in Question 7. The resulting samples are then saved as a raw digital audio file, such as a WAV file.

The quality of the sound card used isn't the only issue that affects capturing audio. The condition of the tape or record player, cables, and the medium itself will, of course, have an effect. Another issue is background noise introduced into the system from the other electronics in the computer. This noise can occasionally be reduced by moving the sound card to a different slot inside the computer to distance it from the other components.

You'll need to use some kind of sound capture software to actually record the audio that is being sent to your sound card. There are a number of excellent programs available that allow capturing, mixing, and audio editing. Many of these programs also include ways to reduce unwanted noise such as clicks and pops. The Web resources I list have links to a large variety of capture software and utilities. However, if your goal is to convert non-CD music sources to MP3 without a lot of hassle, you may simply want to use the audio capture utilities built into some MP3 creation software. For example, MusicMatch Jukebox allows you to record and encode from a source plugged into your sound card. This is usually sufficient if you aren't interested in spending a lot of time tweaking the recordings you make.

Capturing audio from an analog source is a lot more convoluted than ripping it from a CD, but sometimes it's the only option. To learn more about capturing audio, choosing a high-end sound card, or finding the best audio capture software, check out the reviews, discussion areas, and software resource links at these excellent sites:

▶ Hitsquad.com Shareware Music Machine (**www.sonicspot.com**)

▶ HomeRecording.com (**www.homerecording.com**)

11
Ripping and Encoding

Once you've chosen software for ripping and encoding MP3s, and you've made sure you have the necessary computer equipment, you're ready to actually create some MP3s. In this chapter, you'll learn about the most commonly used configuration settings needed when creating MP3s. While AudioCatalyst and MusicMatch will be used in examples throughout this chapter, the basic functionality of many ripping/encoding packages is similar, and these examples can be applied broadly.

Q70 What's this software going to do?

Most combined ripper/encoder programs (see **Question 67**) are very straightforward to use, after they've been installed and configured. For example, when you put a music CD into your CD-ROM drive, both AudioCatalyst and MusicMatch display a list of the tracks on the CD. You simply check off which tracks you want to convert to MP3 files, and then, with a single click, the ripping and encoding processes are started (see **Figure 11.1**).

Ripping and Encoding - Chapter 11

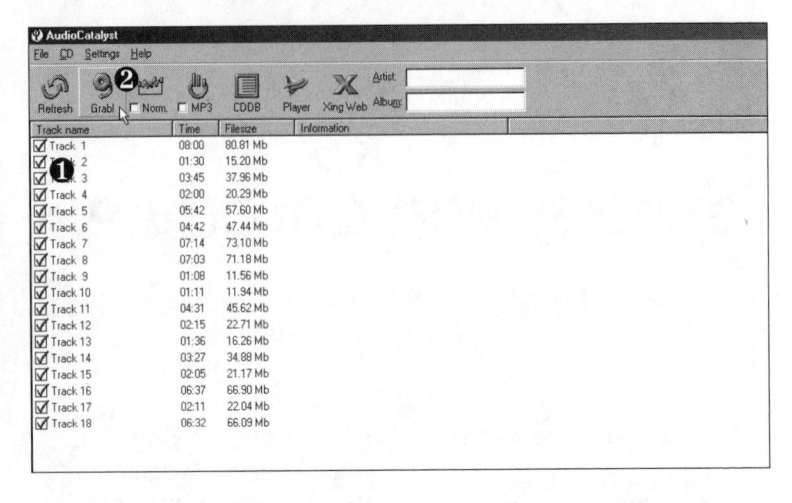

Track name	Time	Filesize
Track 1	08:00	80.81 Mb
Track 2	01:30	15.20 Mb
Track 3	03:45	37.96 Mb
Track 4	02:00	20.29 Mb
Track 5	05:42	57.60 Mb
Track 6	04:42	47.44 Mb
Track 7	07:14	73.10 Mb
Track 8	07:03	71.18 Mb
Track 9	01:08	11.56 Mb
Track 10	01:11	11.94 Mb
Track 11	04:31	45.62 Mb
Track 12	02:15	22.71 Mb
Track 13	01:36	16.26 Mb
Track 14	03:27	34.88 Mb
Track 15	02:05	21.17 Mb
Track 16	06:37	66.90 Mb
Track 17	02:11	22.04 Mb
Track 18	06:32	66.09 Mb

Check off the tracks ❶ and press the Grab! button ❷ to start ripping and encoding in AudioCatalyst.

Figure 11.1 Ripping and Encoding using AudioCatalyst.

However, there are usually a number of configuration options you can set to tweak the resulting MP3 files so they are best suited for what you intend to do with them. Although the default settings are often just fine, you might want to review the settings before you begin. Most programs have similar options, although you might have to review the help file of the program you've chosen to learn exactly how a given option works for that program. In AudioCatalyst, the various configuration options for ripping and encoding are accessible by selecting the items listed in the Settings menu shown in **Figure 11.2**.

http://www.muskalipman.com

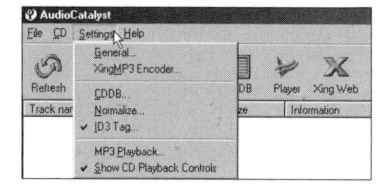

Figure 11.2 AudioCatalyst's Settings Menu

MusicMatch is a little more convenient to configure because it collects almost all the options available for ripping and encoding in one place—the Recording tab of its Settings dialog box, which is found under the Options menu (see **Figures 11.3** and **11.4**).

Figure 11.3 MusicMatch settings are found under the Options menu.

http://www.muskalipman.com

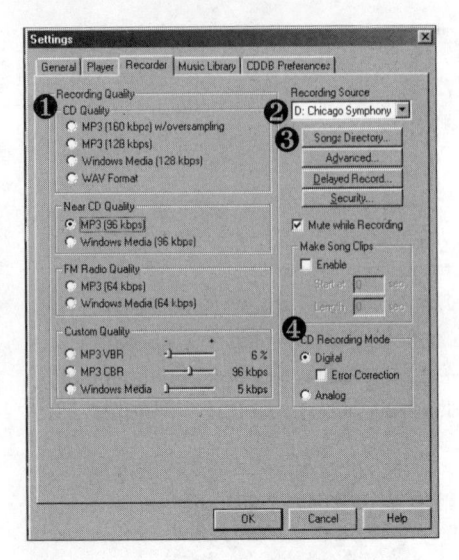

On this Recorder tab, you can choose:

1 Encoding quality

2 Source (eg. rip from a CD or record from a source plugged into the sound card)

3 A directory to store completed MP3s

4 Digital audio extraction or analog extraction

Figure 11.4 Recorder tab of the Settings dialog.

For most ripping and encoding programs, the most important settings you have control over are the following:

▶ Method of audio extraction from CD (digital or analog)

▶ Use of a WAV file intermediate step

▶ Bitrate and method of encoding the MP3

▶ Number of channels that are encoded (stereo or mono)

▶ Normalization
▶ ID3 Tagging of MP3 tracks
▶ Naming and location of finished MP3 files

We'll cover what you can do with these settings in the next several questions.

Q71 Should I use digital or analog as the CD-ROM access method?

Digital extraction is the preferred method of ripping CDs. One major reason for this preference is speed. Analog extraction is done at normal playback speed, whereas digital extraction can often be done several times faster. Another advantage digital extraction has is that it doesn't depend on the quality of your sound card.

> **NOTE**
> AudioCatalyst refers to ASPI and MSCDEX as CD access methods. These are both ways of doing digital extraction. ASPI is the preferred setting because it's usually faster.

Unfortunately, not all CD-ROM drives are capable of *digital audio extraction* (refer back to **Question 68**). Additionally, some CD-ROM drives that are capable of digital extraction might not do a very good job, resulting in pops and clicks in the ripped audio tracks. Sometimes, these noises can be eliminated through *jitter* correction.

http://www.muskalipman.com

> **NOTE**
>
> When using digital extraction, a CD-ROM drive can rip information off a music CD faster than the computer can process it. When this happens, the CD-ROM must pause and then attempt to restart reading exactly where it left off. It turns out that CD-ROM drives were designed in a way that makes it difficult to get this synchronization perfect. The result is that some audio samples from the CD can be doubled up or skipped as they're read. These small imperfections can result in clicks in the ripped audio file. This phenomenon is known as jitter.
>
> Jitter correction is the process of fixing these imperfections, typically using software. It works by making the CD-ROM drive read overlapping sections of the CD track and then matching up the sections and eliminating the overlaps. Because the CD-ROM drive intentionally reads some of the same information more than once, using jitter correction slows down the ripping process. For that reason, jitter correction is typically turned on only when it's needed.
>
> In MusicMatch, jitter correction is turned on by selecting the Error Correction check box.
>
> In AudioCatalyst, there are several ways to enable jitter correction. If you have the ASPI CD access method selected, choose Dynamic Synch Width or one of the Fixed Sync Width rip methods. Using the MSCDEX CD access method also enables jitter correction. If the first combination you try doesn't work, one of the others might.

In analog extraction, the music CD is played back through your sound card and sampled there, just like any other source that was plugged into the line-in jack on your sound card. So, the quality of your sound card affects the quality of the ripped file. Refer back to **Question 69** for more discussion of capturing audio through the sound card. Analog extraction is typically used as a last resort, chosen only when digital extraction (with or without jitter correction) fails.

Q72. Should I rip to a WAV file before encoding a track as an MP3 file?

Many programs allow you to rip CD tracks to WAV files before encoding them as MP3 files. There are several reasons why this might be desirable, including the following:

▶ To burn tracks onto a custom audio CD

▶ When experiencing trouble ripping and encoding at the same time

▶ To be able to turn on normalization (see **Question 74**)

If you intend to create custom CDs with a mix of tracks ripped from several original CDs, you might want to rip directly to WAV. By doing so, the tracks on your new audio CD will be exactly the same as the original. An audio CD created from MP3 files will have the same quality of the MP3 files, which isn't necessarily as good as the original WAV. **Chapter 12**, "How to Get the Most Out of Your MP3 Collection," discusses creating custom audio CDs in more depth.

You might also want to rip to a WAV file if your computer has trouble ripping and encoding at the same time. This is a good possibility if you have an older, less powerful computer or if you have a CD-ROM that can perform DAE at very fast speeds. By completing the ripping and encoding in separate steps, the computer can dedicate all of its resources to each task in turn. However, if your computer isn't having any trouble ripping and encoding at the same time, doing both in a single step is usually faster than doing them separately.

> **TIP**
> When ripping and encoding MP3 files, make sure you've closed all other applications to free up resources for the computer to use.

> **TIP**
>
> Some programs, such as AudioCatalyst, have an Intermediate WAV option that allows you to rip to a WAV file, encode the WAV file as an MP3, and then delete the WAV file automatically. This gives you the benefit of ripping and encoding separately without losing the convenience of not having to be there to start each step.

Q73. What bitrate and encoding method should I use when creating my MP3 files?

The encoding method and bitrate at which you encode your MP3 files affects their faithfulness to the original and the amount of space they take up.

The first choice you have is between the following two encoding methods:

▶ Constant Bitrate Encoding *(CBR)*
▶ Variable Bitrate Encoding *(VBR)*

Constant Bitrate Encoding, the more commonly used method, uses the same bitrate for an entire MP3 file. The advantage of this method is that the size of the finished MP3 can be calculated exactly before encoding it just by knowing the length of the track and the bitrate it will be encoded at. The main disadvantage of CBR is that it requires the encoder to use the same amount of information to represent both complex and very simple sections of audio. In a simple section of audio, such as silence, the encoder must waste bits, although it might not have enough bits later to completely represent an important, complex section of the audio.

Variable Bitrate Encoding attempts to address this shortcoming. It dynamically allocates extra bits during complex sections of the audio track and uses fewer when it can get away with it during simpler sections of the audio. The end result is an MP3 file with a consistent quality level throughout the entire track. VBR's disadvantage is that, due to its nature, it is impossible to predict the size of the finished MP3 file. As a result, some MP3 players have difficulty with VBR-encoded files because they can't determine the play time of the track.

After the encoding method has been selected, the bitrate or quality level must also be chosen. When CBR is used, you can actually specify a bitrate. Most MP3 encoders support the full range of bitrates allowed by MP3 specification, which is from 16kbps to 320kbps. A bitrate of 128kbps is considered to be CD-quality and is the best tradeoff between quality and file size for most applications. A lower bitrate, such as 96 or 112kbps, might be a good choice if file size is particularly important, as it is in portable MP3 players with limited storage capacity. Alternatively, a higher bitrate can be chosen for a higher quality sound, but the file size grows quickly with little discernible quality improvement as the bitrate is raised above 128kbps.

When VBR is chosen as the encoding method, you cannot specify the exact bitrate. However, most encoders do allow you to pick a quality level from a sliding scale. For example, the AudioCatalyst program offers several VBR settings between Low, which is described as near CD-quality similar to CBR encoding at 96kbps, and High, which is compared to the quality of CBR encoding at 192kbps. Consult the documentation of the encoder program you're using to determine its range of VBR settings if you choose that encoding method.

Q74. What is normalization?

Most music CDs are recorded with all of their tracks adjusted to the same peak volume level, usually around 95 percent, so that you don't have to adjust the volume on your stereo in between each track. However, CDs are occasionally recorded with a much lower peak level, and if you convert CDs recorded at different levels to MP3 files and mix up the tracks, you'll be constantly adjusting the playback volume.

The solution to this problem is to normalize all the tracks you rip from CDs to a single peak level. Many ripping programs let you specify a level at which tracks are normalized, and most of these programs recommend a setting between 95 and 100 percent. Some programs, such as AudioCatalyst, allow you to selectively normalize only if the peak level of a given track is significantly different from your specified level. This can be useful if you want to rip borderline cases exactly as they are on the CD.

> **TIP**
> The AudioGrabber (www.audiograbber.com-us.net) ripping and encoding program has even more normalization options, allowing you to adjust both the peak level and the average level of ripped tracks.

Even if you use *normalization* when ripping all of your tracks, if you download MP3 tracks from the Web, you have no guarantee that they've been normalized to the same settings you use. In that situation, you might want to consider an MP3 player that lets you normalize the volume as the finished MP3 tracks are played back. Refer to **Chapter 7**, "Setting Up to Listen," for tips on that subject.

Q75 How can I set the track information that gets displayed by my MP3 player?

Most MP3 encoding programs allow you to save extra information about each track at the end of the MP3 file in a special format called an *ID3 tag*. When this tagging format was first introduced by Eric Kemp in 1996, it included space for the track title, artist, album name, year of release, a short comment, and the genre. The tag format was later modified by Michael Mutschler to squeeze in a value for the track number of the original recording. The original ID3 format was called ID3v1, and the slightly modified format is known as ID3v1.1. Nearly all MP3 players can recognize and display the information stored in these formats.

Some encoders and players, such as MusicMatch, have begun to support a newer revision of these tags known as ID3v2. This format is much more flexible, because it allows the tag to be larger to include more information. It includes more space for the existing descriptions, such as title and artist, as well as completely new information like Web URLs, song lyrics, and album cover graphics.

Check the documentation of the MP3 encoder you're using to learn where to find its ID3 tag editor. Or read on to the next question and you might never have to use it!

Q76 It's annoying to have to type in the descriptive information for each MP3 track I make. Is there a way to get it automatically?

Entering the track title, artist, and other information into the ID3 tag editor for each track on a CD can become quite tedious. Fortunately, there's a free online database, the *CDDB*, which can be accessed by your software to look up the track information for your CDs. The software can then fill in the ID3 tag fields for you. Depending on the program you're using, the CDDB information can be retrieved automatically when you put a new CD into your drive, or you might actually have to press a button to trigger the lookup.

> **NOTE**
> According to the CDDB, it's the largest online CD database. Created in 1993, it has grown to include information on more than 6 million tracks spanning more than 400,000 albums. The CDDB is queried more than 500,000 times per day by people all over the world.
>
> *Source: CDDB homepage (**www.cddb.org**)*

12

How to Get the Most Out of Your MP3 Collection

After you begin ripping your music CDs or downloading MP3 tracks from the Web, you can build up a large collection very quickly. Many people have collections of hundreds or thousands of MP3 tracks. This chapter describes some of the things you can do to take advantage of your growing MP3 collection.

Q77 Can I create regular music CDs from my MP3 collection?

Not everyone is ready to toss out the portable or car CD player in exchange for an MP3 player. Until that time comes, a great way to be able to enjoy the MP3 tracks you've collected is to create your own audio CDs containing your MP3 music. What does it take to make your own music CDs? You need a special kind of CD-ROM drive called a *CD-R* (CD-Recordable) and software that can write to the CD (a process known as *burning* the CD) in the standard audio CD format.

> **NOTE**
> The CD-R writing process is often called burning because the drive uses a laser to burn the information into the colored dye layer of the CD-R disk.

Q78 What features should I consider when buying a CD-R drive?

When they were first introduced, CD-R drives were quite expensive, but now some lower-end models are available for $200 or less. In fact, many new systems come with a CD-R capable CD-ROM drive included.

If your computer doesn't already have a CD-R drive, there are several main features you'll want to compare when shopping for one:

- CD-R versus *CD-RW*/CD-R
- Drive speed
- Internal versus external drives
- Type of interface used
- Buffer size
- Digital Audio Extraction (DAE) capability

CD-R versus CD-RW/CD-R

There are currently two main types of recordable CD-ROM drives available:

- CD-R (CD-Recordable)
- CD-RW (CD-ReWritable)

CD-R drives allow you to permanently record on a blank CD-R disc, whereas CD-RW drives use a different type of disc that can be erased and reused. Most CD-RW drives can also write using CD-R, which is fortunate because CD-RW discs don't work in audio CD players or most computer CD-ROM drives (CD-RW discs require drives with greater sensitivity to read the data). However, CD-RW discs can be read by CD-ROM drives with MultiRead support, because these drives are designed to be sensitive enough to read CD-RW discs. **Table 12.1** shows which drives can read the various types of discs once they've been created.

CD-RW can be a nice feature to have, but the drives and blank discs do cost more. If you think you'll mainly be creating audio CDs and permanent backups, a CD-R drive is probably the most cost-effective choice.

Table 12.1—Which drives will *read* which discs?

	Audio CD	CD-R disc	CD-RW disc
CD player	X	X*	
Typical CD-ROM drives	X	X	
CD-ROM with MultiRead support	X	X	X
CD-R drive	X	X	
CD-RW drive	X	X	X

audio format only

Drive Speed

The speed of the drive you choose determines how quickly you can read from and write to discs. There should be a separate speed listed for both reading and writing (and a separate one for rewriting if it's a CD-RW drive). The faster the drive you choose, the more expensive it is (see **Table 12.2**).

Table 12.2—Time Required to Burn a Full CD-R Disc (650MB)

CD-R Write Speed	Approximate Time Needed
1X	74 min.
2X	37 min.
4X	19 min.
8X	10 min.

http://www.muskalipman.com

Internal versus External Drives

CD-Recordable drives are usually mounted internally in the case of your computer, along with your other drives, but external drives with their own case are also available. An external drive can be a good solution if you don't have any space left in your computer's case, or if you want to be able to use the new drive with more than one computer. However, external drives cost more.

Type of Interface

There are several different types of interfaces between the CD-R drive and the computer itself. The mounting location (internal or external) you choose, as well as whether you have a PC or Mac, limits which interfaces are available for you. The main interface choices are as follows:

- **IDE/EIDE/ATAPI**—IDE/EIDE/ATAPI is the cheapest and most common choice for PCs, but it requires an internal drive and is slower than SCSI. It doesn't work with Macs.

- **SCSI**—Allows fast transfer speeds more reliably than IDE/EIDE/ATAPI, but is also more expensive. It requires the purchase of an SCSI adapter card that must be installed inside your computer. It's available for both PCs and Macs and can be used with an internal or external drive.

- **Parallel Port**—A parallel port interface requires an external drive and works only with PCs. It offers convenience and portability but is slow (you may have difficulty burning at speeds greater than 2X with a drive that uses a parallel port interface).

- **USB**—USB is a newer interface type that is becoming available as a choice for CD recording drives. It can be used with any PC or Mac that has a USB port. USB drives are external and can typically burn reliably at 4X speeds.

Buffer Size

CD-Recordable drives have memory built in, which holds the data just before it's written to the disc. This memory is referred to as the cache or *buffer*. The computer must try to keep this buffer from running empty, a situation called a *buffer underrun*, or else the laser used to write to the disc will lose its place and the recording process will have to be restarted with a new disk. The larger the buffer size of a drive, the less likely there will be a buffer underrun. The faster you'd like to burn a disc, the larger buffer you will need. To burn at 4X speeds look for a drive with at least a 2MB buffer. Many new drives come with a 4MB buffer, which will keep buffer underruns to a minimum at speeds greater than 4X.

Digital Audio Extraction Capability

If you're going to buy a new CD-ROM drive, make sure it supports digital audio extraction (DAE) so you can rip music CDs to create MP3 files.

> **TIP**
> If you'd like to learn more about CD-R, check out the comp.publish.cdrom newsgroup's CD-Recordable FAQ at **www.faqs.org/faqs/cdrom/cd-recordable/part1/**.

Q79 What's the process for creating my own music CD?

You will use the CD creation software that came with your CD-R drive to make your own audio CD, but first you need to convert your MP3 tracks back to WAV format. If you have the CD that the MP3 track was created from, you'll get the best quality on your new CD if you use the WAV file that was ripped originally rather than converting the MP3 back to WAV. (Refer to **Question 71**.)

One of the easiest ways to convert your MP3s to WAV format is using the Winamp player and its Disk Writer plug-in (see **Figure 12.1**). Here's what you need to do:

▶ Open the Winamp Preferences (press Ctrl-P)

▶ View the output plug-in choices by clicking on Output in the left window of the Preferences dialog and then select Nullsoft Disk Writer as the output plug-in.

▶ While you're still in the Preferences dialog box, you can specify where the WAV files will be written using the Configure button. Make sure you have lots of free space on the drive that you specify for the WAV files—they're going to be big! You'll need around 700MB of free space for enough WAV files to fill an audio CD.

▶ Close the Preferences dialog.

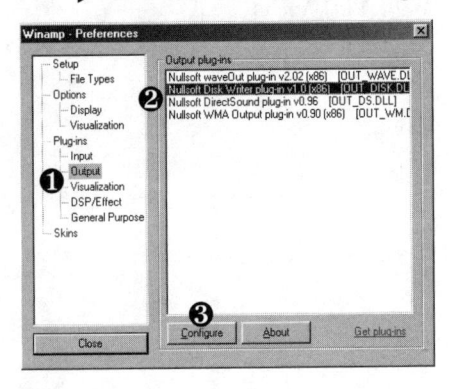

❶ Select Plug-Ins > Output
❷ Highlight the Nullsoft Disk Writer plug-in
❸ Click Configure to select a location for the WAV files

Figure 12.1 Configure Winamp to use the Nullsoft Disk Writer plug-in to convert MP3 files to WAV.

▶ Next, build a playlist of the MP3 tracks you want to convert to WAV. As you build the playlist, remember that the music CD you're going to create can hold a maximum of 74 minutes of audio.

▶ Click the Play button to create the WAV files. Instead of hearing the tracks through your sound card, they are written to the location you specified.

▶ When you're done writing out the WAV files, don't forget to reconfigure Winamp's preferences to use Nullsoft waveOut as the output plug-in. The waveOut plug-in directs the audio to your sound card rather than to a WAV file on your hard drive. If you forget to change the output plug-in back to waveOut, you won't hear anything the next time you try to listen to your MP3 files!

After you have the tracks for your audio CD in WAV format, it's time to write them onto the blank CD-R disc using your CD creation software.

Nearly all audio CD writing programs work basically the same way. The main steps are typically as follows:

▶ Select which WAV files to include on your CD
▶ Set the write speed
▶ Select from disk closing options
▶ Test and/or burn the CD-R disk

Many CD writing software packages, including the popular Adaptec Easy CD Creator, will walk you step by step through the necessary configuration (see **Figure 12.2**).

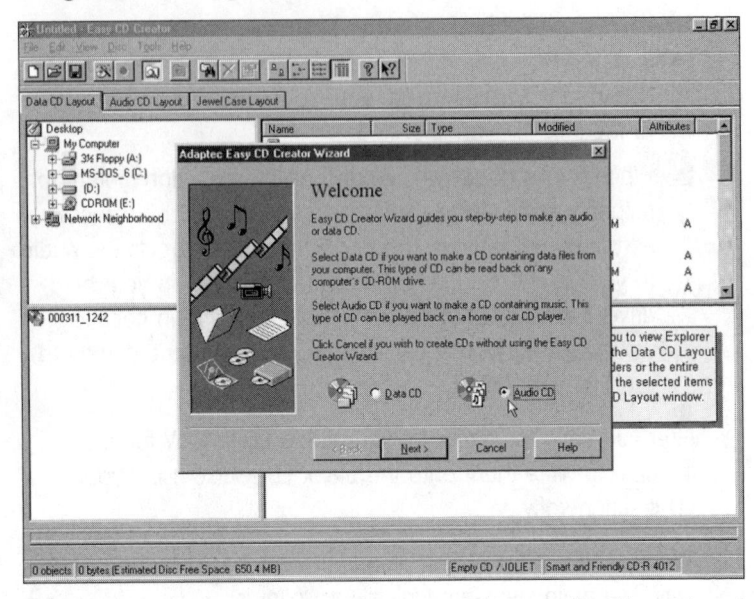

Figure 12.2 The Adaptec Easy CD Creator program's wizard will walk you through the steps needed to create your CD.

Select WAVs to Include

After you start up the CD writing software, you'll need to tell it what WAV files you want included and what order you want them in on your new CD. Most programs give you some indication of how much play time is left open on the CD so that you don't try to add more audio than will fit.

Select Write Speed

Most programs let you control the speed at which your drive writes the CD-R disc. The faster the speed you choose, the less time it will take to burn the CD. However, attempting to burn at faster speeds will occasionally result in a buffer underrun error, and you'll have to start the burn over with a new disc. Fortunately, most CD writing software allows you to test your system's performance and make a recommendation on what speed you should try.

Select from Disc Closing Options

Your CD writing software might give you several options for what the drive does to the disc when it's done recording. Following are the most common options:

▶ **Leave Session Open**—If you want to be able to add tracks to the audio CD later, this is the best setting. However, you cannot listen to the CD in a regular CD player until the session is closed.

▶ **Close Session and Leave Disc Open**—This is a good choice if you want to be able to listen to the audio tracks on your CD in a music CD player, but you aren't ready to write-protect it yet. Any leftover space can be used during a later session. However, regular CD players can only read the tracks in the first session on a CD.

▶ **Close Disc**—Close Disc write-protects the CD so that nothing more can be written to it after the current session has finished.

▶ **Disc-at-Once**—Disc-At-Once burns the entire CD in one pass and leaves out the normal two-second delay between tracks. It automatically closes the disc.

Test and Burn the Disc

After you've configured your CD writing software, you're ready to burn (but hopefully not crash and burn!). Many times, the program has an option to test your configuration to make sure the burn will be successful. This test usually consists of the drive doing everything it would do during a normal burn except turning on the laser. Doing a test before you burn a disc is a very good idea, at least until you've successfully burned several discs and have a good idea of the performance of your setup. After you know what settings work consistently, you should turn off the testing stage (which slows down the burning process).

> **TIP**
> When you're burning a CD, it's best to close all the other applications that are running and avoid using your computer. That way, nothing interferes with the data transfer process, and you are less likely to experience a buffer underrun. Junk CDs resulting from buffer underruns or other problems during the burning process are often called *coasters*, because they're not good for much besides setting your drink on!

Q80 What are music servers and how can I set up my own?

The stereo system of the future will probably be as much computer as stereo, although you probably won't think of it as a computer. With it, you'll be able to surf the Web for new music and listen to radio stations, and, of course, you'll never have to change another CD! It will be flexible enough to play many formats of music, from MP3 to the latest and greatest format, with just an upgrade of your stereo's software. You might think of it as a kind of music server for your home and car.

We might not be quite to that point yet, but some people are leading the charge and creating their own system using a computer plugged in to a regular stereo system. With powerful computers available for less than $1,000 and the availability of cheap, very large hard drives that can hold gigabytes of MP3 files, the music server can be created today.

The quickest and easiest way to create your own MP3 music server is to simply run cables from the line out jack of your computer's sound card to your stereo and use a jukebox-style MP3 player to manage your MP3 collection. However, unless your computer is normally near your stereo system, or you have a spare computer you can dedicate to your stereo, this might not be very convenient. Very long cables are also prone to introducing an annoying hum, which makes this option less attractive.

The MP3 Anyware product (**www.x10.com/mp3_x10/mp3_anywhere.htm**), which sells for around $100, tries to address some of these problems by going wireless. It consists of a transmitter that plugs in to your computer's sound card, and a receiver that plugs in to your stereo system. The audio from your computer is broadcast through walls up to 100 feet, according to the manufacturer. It even includes a universal remote that can control your stereo components as well as popular MP3 players such as Winamp and MusicMatch.

If you want to ditch the computer altogether, there are a couple of options becoming available. The AudioReQuest (**www.audiorequest.com**) is a home stereo component that plays MP3s from CD-ROM or from its own hard drive (see **Figure 12.3**). You can use the AudioReQuest to convert your music CDs to MP3, or you can download your existing MP3 collection to it through its parallel port interface. The AudioReQuest connects to your stereo system for playback and provides onscreen playlist editing through your TV.

Figure 12.3 The AudioReQuest adds MP3 to your existing entertainment system.

The Kerbango Internet Radio (**www.kerbango.com**), shown in **Figure 12.4**, can be used to tune in Net radio stations provided through the Kerbango Tuning Service when it's connected to the Internet through your ISP (it can plug in to a phone line or a home ethernet network). The Kerbango has built-in speakers, but you can also connect it to a stereo system using its line out jack. If you have a home network, you can use the Kerbango to play MP3 files stored on your PC.

Figure 12.4 The Kerbango Internet Radio tunes in Net radio stations and can play MP3 files.

Q81 Can I create my own Net radio station to stream MP3s?

Have you ever wanted to be the DJ or maybe a radio talk show host? Perhaps you'd like to set up a radio station dedicated to your own band!

Running your own Net radio station is one of the coolest things you can do with MP3. It puts you in control of all aspects of your station's operation—from picking the tunes to promoting the station.

Getting your station set up takes some effort. This chapter will introduce some of the major topics you need to know about to get started with Net radio and will point you in the right direction to learn more. You may also want to consider reading the book *Online Broadcasting Power!* by Ben Sawyer and Dave Greely (Muska & Lipman ©2000, ISBN 096628898X), which covers Net radio in detail.

To set up a Net radio station, you'll need to do the following:

▶ Select and install Net radio station software
▶ Consider Webcasting legal requirements

Choosing and Installing Net Radio Station Software

The first thing you need to run your own Net radio station is the server software that actually streams your music or programs to your listeners. In addition to this server software, you also need a program that combines the live or recorded audio you're broadcasting and gets that to the server software so it can be sent out to the world.

http://www.muskalipman.com

These two programs work together to allow you to control the number of users who can connect at a given time and the quality level of the audio you broadcast. Each of the various server/player packages that are available has its own guidelines for its configuration settings, most of which are based on the speed of the connection between your server and the Internet.

Good MP3 streaming packages include the following:

► **Nullsoft SHOUTcast (www.shoutcast.com)**—SHOUTcast is an MP3 streaming server developed by the creators of Winamp. Not surprisingly, it uses the Winamp player (along with some utilities) as a source for its audio stream. Listeners can tune in to your broadcast using MP3 players such as Winamp, MusicMatch Jukebox, and others.

SHOUTcast is free for nonprofit, noncommercial use, or it can be licensed for other use for $299 per server.

Directions for installing and configuring the server software as well as the Winamp player components of the server are described at the SHOUTcast Web site.

► **Xing StreamWorks MP3 Server (www.xingtech.com/ mp3/ streamworks)**—StreamWorks MP3 Server is a free streaming server developed by Xing, the makers of the AudioCatalyst program. It broadcasts a stream to up to fifty concurrent listeners. The audio stream is provided to the server software using the Xing MP3 Live! Encoder.

The StreamWorks MP3 Server is simpler to set up than SHOUTcast, but your listeners must use the StreamWorks Player (also a free download) to hear your broadcast.

> **TIP**
> An alternative to these streaming MP3 servers is the RealNetworks Basic Server G2, which lets you stream to listeners in the RealAudio format rather than MP3. A version that supports up to 25 streams can be downloaded for free at the RealNetworks Web site: **www.realnetworks.com/products/servers/basic.html**.

Complying with Webcasting laws

After you have a server set up, there are a number of legal and licensing considerations you need to be aware of, unless you're broadcasting only your own original content.

The Recording Industry Association of America (RIAA) has a good introduction to licensing of music for Web broadcasting at **www.riaa.com/weblic/weblic.htm**. The RIAA's FAQ on Web Licensing describes the steps that must be taken to comply with current copyright law.

> **TIP**
> If you'd like to have your own Net radio station but don't want to have to deal with setting up the software yourself, you may want to consider a service like Live365.com (**www.live365.com**). Live365 allows you to upload up to 365MB of MP3 files and put together your own playlist for the station. This is a great option if your computer isn't connected to the Internet all the time but you still want your station to be broadcasting. Live365.com also has an option that allows you to do live broadcasting from your computer.
>
> As long as you follow the broadcasting rules provided by Live365.com, the company takes care of musical composition performance royalties through ASCAP, BMI, and SESAC, as well as sound recording licenses. This cuts out some of the hassles and lets you concentrate on making your station the best it can be!

13
Distributing Your Own Music Using MP3

In previous chapters, you've seen just how easy it is to *find* about any kind of music from any type of band or artist. But perhaps *you're* the unsigned artist who wants to take advantage of MP3 and the Web to get your music noticed. This chapter covers questions you might have about how to use MP3 to promote your own music.

Q82. How can I use MP3 to get my own music out to the world?

There are a number of ways to start getting your music out where lots of people will be able to hear it. Some of the best ways to promote yourself online using MP3 include the following:

▶ Set up a Web site with downloadable tracks
▶ Submit your songs to Net radio stations
▶ Create your own Net radio station

We'll go into each of these in more depth in this chapter.

Remember that using MP3 is just one step in promotion. You still have to get people excited about your material! One of the nice things about using MP3 and the Web is that you can do as much or as little as you want. However, the more effort you put into online promotion, the more likely you'll get something out of it.

Q83 How can I set up a free personal or band homepage?

The easiest way to set up a Web site for yourself is to use one of the several popular MP3 portal sites that offer free Web sites for artists. These sites encourage artists to set up pages and provide free tracks so they can attract more visitors to their site. Many sites even volunteer their help selling music and other merchandise to lend unsigned artists a hand. Here are several MP3 portals that provide free Web sites for artists to post MP3 downloads.

IUMA (www.iuma.com)

IUMA is a site that offers a free Web site where you can post your band's bio, pictures, and sample tracks. IUMA also includes a collection of tips for promoting yourself, both online and offline, as well as a newsletter with music industry advice. The site tracks not only the number of downloads your music gets, but also the number of times someone looks at your Web site. Artists get paid 25 percent of any banner advertising revenue collected by IUMA for their personal site. If you have CDs you want to sell from your band's IUMA Web site, IUMA also provides that service.

MP3.com (www.mp3.com)

MP3.com is one of the premier artist community sites and is one of the most popular MP3 sites on the Web (which makes it a good place for *you* to be seen!). In addition to allowing you to create your own Web site within MP3.com, with band info, pictures, and downloadable tracks, MP3.com can create DAM CDs for you to sell from your page of the site. MP3.com also has sponsored promotions that pay cash according to the number of downloads of your music.

Riffage.com (www.riffage.com)

Riffage.com is another good artist community site with a lot of benefits for artists. Artists can create a personalized page with biographies, pictures, schedules, and downloadable tracks. To get your music on the site, you can upload it, transfer it from another Web site (handy if you have a slow Internet connection), or mail in a copy of a CD, which Riffage rips for you. Tracks can be set up to be free downloads, or you can charge for them. Riffage will also sell your band's CDs, T-shirts, stickers, and other promotional items through its site. Artists receive 85 percent of the money from downloads and other merchandise.

RollingStone.com (www.rollingstone.com)

RollingStone.com encourages artists to submit tracks to be included in their MP3 and More free download directory. Artists can also create a band information page with bios, pictures, tour schedules, links to other Web sites, and a listing of the songs they've uploaded. The site also provides stats on how many people have downloaded your music. The tracks that are submitted to RollingStone.com are reviewed by the editors, who regularly post their favorites for special recognition on the site.

You can certainly set up band Web sites at more than one of the artist communities, but you might also choose to concentrate most of your attention on one or two. Pick the site or sites that you like best for finding music. Chances are, those people who are looking for music will have similar feelings. If you create a site, make sure you keep it up-to-date with new pictures, performance dates, and anything else you can think of to make people want to come back again and again. Also, be sure to market your online sites on your printed promotional material.

http://www.muskalipman.com

Q84. How can I set up a more customized Web site for my band?

If you aren't content with the templates provided by the free artist communities, you can create a custom Web site elsewhere. Most of the free Web sites provided by MP3 portals can link to your custom site, if you want to have a custom site but still have the benefit of being discovered at the MP3 portal site.

One option is to build a site at a free hosting service such as Tripod (**www.tripod.lycos.com**) or GeoCities (**geocities.yahoo.com**). These services let you construct a much more elaborate and customized Web site, but you might have to learn HTML, the language used to create Web pages. You can find hundreds of companies with servers to host your custom Web site; some will even help you build it. Look in the Web Services category of Yahoo! for a long listing of companies that do this type of work.

Q85. How can I take advantage of Net radio to promote myself?

Net radio is another great way to get your music heard by people all over the world. For example, you can create a Live365.com station featuring artists and music you're influenced by and mix in your own music. Remember that you must follow the rules specified for the Webcasting statutory license except for your own music (see **Question 25** and **Question 81**). Another idea is to Webcast a recording of some of your live performances or have someone interview you. Be creative and don't forget to throw in a couple plugs for yourself!

Another way to use Net radio is to get stations run by others to play your music. Try e-mail or chatting with the DJs of Net radio stations you like—they might be willing to give your music a listen, and if they like it, they might add it to their playlist.

Q86 What are some good resources for musicians who are interested in digital audio distribution?

The MP3 portal communities discussed earlier in this chapter are an excellent place to find helpful advice and information for musicians, even if you don't set up a Web site at each of them. Many of them have regular postings and columns just for people like you.

These sites are also a good starting point for more information:

MusicDish (www.musicdish.com)

MusicDish is an in-depth and authoritative site covering the music industry and the Web's influences on it. It features news and editorials, interviews, music industry surveys, and reviews. The site also includes the MusicDish Genome Project, a large collection of links to music resources on the Web.

Webnoize (www.webnoize.com)

Webnoize is another great source for digital music news, interviews, and resources. However, although some content is available for free, you must pay a subscription fee for full access to the site.

HomeRecording.com (www.homerecording.com)

This is a site with an extensive collection of resources for those who record or mix music at home, including a lot of information on MP3 and digital audio. Check out the Home Recording frequently asked questions at **www.homerecording.com/homerecfaq.html.**

Q87 How can I get my music noticed by the industry using MP3?

Well, one good way to start is by having lots of fans download your tracks! If you rise to the top of the charts of the MP3 artist communities, you stand a better chance of being noticed by the right people. Some of the MP3 portals occasionally run contests where winners get picked up by record companies.

A good site to check out if you're trying to get a recording deal is Jimmy and Doug's Farmclub.com **(www.farmclub.com)**. Music that is uploaded to this site gets a listen from an A&R (artist and repertoire) professional, and the goal of the site is to sign independent artists to record contracts. Undoubtedly, the way major record companies find great new bands will include this type of discovery more and more as the digital music revolution continues.

Q88. Can I distribute a cover of someone else's song as an MP3?

If you record a cover of a song and want to distribute it as an MP3 download, you must obtain a mechanical license that covers the copies you make. (See **Question 21**, "Can I put MP3 files on my Web page?" for more on musical work copyrights.) Mechanical licenses cover copies on physical media, like CDs, as well as digital files, like MP3s. As long as the musical work already has been released by someone else, you can obtain the mechanical license by paying a royalty rate set by law (currently 7.55 cents per copy for most songs). Mechanical licensing is often administered on the copyright holder's behalf by the Harry Fox Agency **(www.nmpa.org/hfa.html)**.

You might also need to obtain a performance license for the musical work from one of the performance rights organizations like BMI, ASCAP, or SESAC. If you're distributing the song through one of the major services like IUMA or Riffage, you might want to check with them to see if they have a blanket license to cover their whole site. As with any legal matter, if you have any questions, it's probably best to consult with an experienced music licensing professional.

Section 5

MP3 and the Future of Digital Audio

14

Where We Are Headed

Q89 What trends will influence the future of digital audio?

The combination of digital audio and the Internet are profoundly changing the way we think about acquiring and listening to music, and the MP3 movement is just the beginning. Over the next several years, we'll see even more rapid changes driven by digital audio and several major trends.

Proliferation of MP3 and related digital audio-capable devices and integration into other mainstream audio equipment

The first portable MP3 players, like Diamond Multimedia's Rio and Saehan's MPMan, began to reach the market near the end of 1998, and a second wave of players started appearing throughout 1999. The earliest generation players were fairly expensive and offered MP3 playback only, although in 1999 some players began to have portable recording features, FM radio tuners, and better LCD screens. This year promises to be the year when portable players will take off with consumers, and by 2001, basic models should be available for less than $100.

Big-name consumer electronics producers like Sony, Casio, RCA, and Phillips will try to catch up to the computer peripheral companies and other, lesser known brands that have dominated the market early on. As competition between manufacturers heats up, prices should decrease and the features of players should continue to improve. At the January 2000 Consumer Electronics Show, an industry trade show, a wide variety of portable MP3 players were shown by manufacturers. These included devices that can play both regular music CDs and CDs that hold 10-plus hours of MP3 files; devices that can hold as many as 150 CD-quality albums; and even a wristwatch with a built-in MP3 player. Devices like these do more than just match the functionality of current portable cassette and CD players—they drive the MP3 movement and digital audio revolution.

MP3 will also continue to push its way into the home and car audio markets with increasing availability of audio components that support the format. There will be a demand for in-dash digital audio car stereos, combination DVD/CD/MP3 home audio components, and even stereo components that are basically easy-to-use, dedicated personal computers for playing digital audio. The latter of these, the stereo PC, will eventually be the most useful and convenient for consumers, because it can be upgraded to support new formats, hold hundreds of albums, and transfer music to portable players. Many of these home audio components, like the Kerbango Internet Radio discussed in **Question 80** and the AudioRamp iRad-s shown in **Figure 14.1**, will connect directly to the Internet, making it possible to download digital audio files directly from the source and listen to Net radio stations. You will still be able to use general purpose personal computers to listen to digital audio, but the MP3 revolution will no longer depend on them.

Figure 14.1 MP3 players designed for the home, like the AudioRamp iRad-s (**www.audioramp.com**), will make it easier for consumers to enjoy the music they download.

More bandwidth and easier access to digital audio content

The availability of high-speed Internet access to the home through phone lines, cable systems, and wireless networks will dramatically increase acceptance of digital audio technology like MP3 downloads and Net radio stations. The increasing ease at which people will be able to download digital audio will drive piracy of music to new levels unless the major record labels provide better legitimate ways for consumers to get the music in the ways and formats they want. For this reason, availability of *bandwidth* is likely to drive availability of more content, including content supplied from mainstream labels and independent artists and labels.

The January 2000 announcement of a merger between Internet service provider AOL and media giant Time Warner is a great example of this trend. AOL wants to provide its users with more content, including the music owned by Time Warner's family of record companies. Additionally, AOL can provide faster access to its members by using cable modems and Time Warner's existing cable network.

"Pervasive" computing

Pervasive computing is the idea that, in the not-so-distant future, we'll have access to the capabilities of a computer connected to the Internet no matter where we are—in the car, in the living room, or walking through the mall with a handheld device or phone. This trend will have a large impact on the digital audio revolution by giving people the ability to find new music or enjoy what they already own, no matter where they are.

For example, imagine a portable MP3 player that doesn't need any storage—it simply connects to the Internet directly and plays the music stored on your home stereo system or tunes in your favorite Net radio stations. This type of device will be available sooner than you think. Ericsson has shown a prototype phone with an add-on MP3 player that can play through the same stereo headset you use to take your calls (see **Figure 14.2**). Although the current prototype player uses onboard storage rather than connecting to the Internet though the phone, such technology is on its way. For example, automakers General Motors and Ford have announced relationships with AOL and Yahoo, respectively, to work on Internet-enabled vehicles.

Figure 14.2 This prototype wireless phone/MP3 player hints of what is to come with pervasive computing.

Development of new digital audio formats and more secure means of distribution

A number of digital audio formats have been developed that are technically superior to MP3 in their compression and audio quality, but they haven't yet taken MP3's place as the *lingua franca* of digital audio. One reason they haven't taken over is that these formats often require more powerful computers and devices to encode and decode the music. However, given that computer power is increasing, and prices decreasing, that will not be the most important reason in the long term. The more important reason these formats haven't overtaken MP3 is their proprietary nature. Consumers have so far been unwilling to accept proprietary alternative formats that don't work with as many software and portable players. Many of these proprietary formats also use cumbersome security schemes, which make them less attractive to convenience-minded consumers who want to listen to their music on multiple devices without major hassles. Some of the currently available alternative digital audio formats are discussed in **Question 91**.

The aforementioned security schemes used with some of the current digital audio formats are a result of the music industry's attempts to retain control over the distribution of its content, to protect its copyrights and livelihood. A *digital rights management (DRM)* system tracks licensing and ownership of songs using unique identifiers embedded in the music called *digital watermarks*; it then prevents unauthorized copying or playing of the song using that information. The listener or the listener's player must provide the key or identification needed to unlock the secure audio file.

> **NOTE**
>
> A digital watermark consists of bits spread throughout a file that include owner and licensing information specific to that particular copy of the file. The information stored in a watermark can be used by digital rights management systems to track and prevent unauthorized use of the file. For digital audio watermarking, the watermark must be inaudible when the file is played and must be able to withstand changes to the file, such as conversion between different digital audio formats. The watermark must be capable of being read, but it must also be very difficult to remove.

The *Secure Digital Music Initiative (SDMI)* is a project initiated by the recording industry that takes on the task of providing a standard framework that would allow secure delivery of digital audio using digital rights management schemes without limiting itself to a particular digital audio format. If SDMI can produce such a framework, it might help secure digital audio formats compete against unsecured MP3 by making them compatible across more devices. However, SDMI has been criticized for moving too slowly and allowing MP3 to become more firmly entrenched. SDMI's efforts are discussed in more detail in **Question 90**.

Even if SDMI is successful in generating a framework for secure digital audio delivery, it isn't guaranteed success with consumers. Many feel that concerns about personal privacy will stall acceptance of secure systems that require unique identifiers embedded in the music and identification of the user when they listen to a song. Consumers are also unlikely to accept any system that is less convenient than an unsecured one, where they don't have to worry about entering passwords and don't have any difficulty in transferring their music between their own players. Even if a secure framework does catch on, there will still be people who find ways to disable it.

New models of music distribution

Digital audio and the Internet have already begun to make major changes to music distribution models, such as letting consumers pick only the tracks they want rather than an entire album. As the technology driving the trends we've just discussed progresses, even more choices will become available.

Pay-per-listen systems might charge a very small amount each time you listen to a song on your stereo or portable player. Or a secure distribution framework might allow a song to be played for free in degraded quality, with the full level of quality available when payment is made. A subscription model might allow access to specific artists or albums whenever you want. It will be interesting to see if any of these, or other new distribution models, become successful in the new connected age.

Q90 What is SDMI and what has been accomplished?

The Secure Digital Music Initiative, or SDMI, is a forum for members of recording, consumer electronics, and computer technology industries to develop a standard framework for secure music distribution and use. Implementation of the framework in software and audio hardware is voluntary, and using the framework does not limit the device to a particular digital audio format. In fact, SDMI-compliant software and devices can also play unsecured formats, such as MP3, if the manufacturer chooses to include that functionality in the player.

The SDMI forum was established in December 1998 primarily because of the recording industry's concern that the lack of a secure means of distribution would prevent it from keeping control over its product. By early 2000, more than 120 companies and organizations were participating in SDMI. However, SDMI has been criticized by some for not representing the interests of small independent labels and unsigned bands.

http://www.muskalipman.com

The first results of the SDMI effort cover portable devices and were published in July 1999. The specification describes the implementation of SDMI occurring in two phases. During Phase I, devices that follow the SDMI framework will be allowed to play files whether they are secured or unsecured. After Phase II begins, players must be upgraded to Phase II compliance to be able to read digital watermarks embedded in SDMI-compliant music and must use that information to be able to screen out pirated copies. If the players are not upgraded to Phase II compliance, they will still be able to play Phase I-compliant music, but they will be unable to play new Phase II content. Unsecured formats such as MP3 will remain playable even after Phase II begins.

Opponents of SDMI argue that the effort will be a flop with consumers because of:

▶ Consumer confusion over SDMI-compliant formats
▶ Restrictions on copying audio files

Because SDMI is a security framework and doesn't specify a particular audio format, there will likely be multiple SDMI-compliant formats available. These formats won't be interchangeable between portable players and software, which could be confusing to consumers who see the SDMI mark on a product and assume it will work in their SDMI-compliant player. Another problem is that consumers used to being able to easily copy their MP3 or other unsecured audio files with no restrictions might see little incentive to go for an SDMI-compliant player that limits them. Finally, even SDMI-compliant players will be able to play pirated music—it just has to be in an unsecured format like MP3. Because it is quite easy to convert any audio, including that in a secured format, to MP3 by re-recording it, it seems unlikely that

SDMI will prevent piracy. Opponents of SDMI point to this and ask why things should be made more complicated when the people who would steal music still will be able to.

By the end of 2000, we should have a good idea of whether SDMI will be successful or fail. Even if SDMI does bomb, it might help get additional legitimate content into the marketplace by making the major labels feel somewhat safer.

Q91 What other digital audio formats are out there?

Although MP3 is currently the dominating force in digital audio, it will inevitably be replaced by new technology that is far superior. A number of audio coding methods already produce smaller files with equal or better audio quality than MP3. It remains to be seen how long MP3 will be able to withstand challenges from these or other formats.

Formats that currently compete with MP3 include:

- AAC
- ATRAC3
- a2b music
- EPAC
- Liquid Audio
- RealAudio
- VQF
- Windows Media
- AudioAAC

Like MP3, *Advanced Audio Coding (AAC)* is an audio encoding scheme specified by the MPEG-2 standard. Although it is part of the MPEG-2 standard, it is not compatible with the MPEG Layer scheme (see **Chapter 1,** "MP3—The Format") or MP3. AAC was designed by researchers from a number of companies and can be licensed from Dolby Laboratories.

AAC encoding is more efficient than MP3, resulting in smaller file sizes for audio of similar quality. AAC can also provide many more audio channels than MP3, as well as a wider range of sampling rates for better sound quality than is possible with MP3.

Although AAC by itself has not yet been widely used, it has been used as the basis for several proprietary secure formats, and it will be used in the audio portion of the MPEG-4 standard.

The FAQ at the MPEG Audio Web site (**www.tnt.uni-hannover.de/project/mpeg/audio**) is a good source for more technical details on the AAC format.

ATRAC3

Sony's *Adaptive Transform Acoustic Coding 3 (ATRAC3)* format is an improved version of the ATRAC encoding scheme used by MiniDisc players. It achieves nearly the same level of compression and sound quality as MP3 at the same bitrate. Currently, the ATRAC3 format is primarily used by Sony's portable players. Sony has said that ATRAC3 will be SDMI compliant.

a2b music

The *a2b* music format is a proprietary, secure music distribution system developed by AT&T Labs. Because its compression is based on AAC, its files are smaller and can be of higher quality than MP3. The a2b system also includes encryption and a policy manager that controls the licensing of a particular song, including options like how long the song may be played, number of plays allowed, or outright purchase. Tracks in the a2b format will work only on a single computer. Several of the major labels have worked with a2b music, but the format has never really taken off. The a2b music player and additional information on the format can be found at **www.a2bmusic.com.**

EPAC

Lucent Technologies claims its Enhanced Perceptual Audio Coder (EPAC) is indistinguishable from a CD at 11:1 compression, which makes it similar to or slightly better than MP3. EPAC hasn't yet become as popular as some other audio formats, although Maycom, which manufactures the I-Jam portable MP3 player, has licensed the design for an EPAC player from Lucent's partner, e.Digital. The EPAC format will be SDMI compliant.

Liquid Audio

Liquid Audio is another AAC-based proprietary format that incorporates an encryption-based security system. It will follow the SDMI specification.

Liquid Audio has been gaining momentum in the marketplace and will likely be a contender among other SDMI-compliant formats. A number of manufacturers have announced portable players that will support the Liquid Audio format. Also, Liquid Audio has announced that it will work with AOL to add Liquid Audio support to the popular Winamp audio player software. A number of major and independent labels have released tracks in Liquid Audio format. For more information, check out the Liquid Audio Web site at **www.liquidaudio.com.**

RealAudio

RealNetworks has been a pioneer in the streaming of audio and video. The company's *RealAudio* format still holds a major share of the streaming multimedia market, although Windows Media has been catching up. Many people feel RealAudio compares favorably with MP3 at high bitrates, but the format's use is really targeted toward low bitrate streaming.

http://www.muskalipman.com

VQF (TwinVQ)

The *VQF* format is the much-shortened name for Transform-domain Weighted Interleave Vector Quantization format, also sometimes called TwinVQ. It was developed by Nippon Telegraph and Telephone (NTT) and produces audio files with better compression and better sound quality than MP3. However, compared to MP3, VQF requires substantially greater time for the encoding process. Support for VQF has waned as of late, but MPEG-4 audio will incorporate the technology. Check **www.vqf.com** for more resources on VQF.

Windows Media Audio

Windows Media Audio (WMA) is part of Microsoft's Windows Media audio and video software, which includes a digital rights management system to secure the files. WMA quality remains quite high even at low bitrates, and Microsoft claims WMA can reproduce CD-quality audio as low as 64kbps, or roughly twice the compression of MP3. WMA is a downloadable format, and in conjunction with Microsoft's Advanced Streaming Format (ASF), WMA can also be streamed to listeners. In fact, Windows Media competes directly with the more established RealAudio format and is quickly gaining in popularity. Many portable devices already support WMA, and the format is sure to be a major player in the future of digital audio. See the Windows Media Web site at **www.microsoft.com/windows/windowsmedia** for more on WMA.

Q92 Is MPEG working on any new standards?

The MPEG working group of the ISO has been continuing its work to define standards for video and audio. It is working on two different standards: MPEG-4 and MPEG-7.

MPEG-4

MPEG-4 is intended to be an all-purpose multimedia standard for such applications as digital television, computer-generated graphics, and interactive multimedia. It can be used either as a downloadable format or it can be streamed. Although MPEG-4 covers both video and audio, we'll concentrate only on the audio portion.

MPEG-4 Audio works much differently than the earlier MPEG-1 and MPEG-2 standards. It provides a way to represent units of audio content as media objects that, when combined, make up the whole. For example, the audio portion for a scene of a movie soundtrack might be composed of several media objects: a person speaking in the foreground, the sound of footsteps, and the sound of traffic in the background. These MPEG-4 objects might be natural sounds, such as recorded music or voice, or they can be synthesized sounds based on descriptions. Each of these objects would be represented separately and distinctly in the MPEG-4 representation, which allows some very powerful manipulation to be done on the receiving end. MPEG-4 uses different methods of encoding for natural sound, including AAC and VQF, depending on the bitrate specified for a particular audio object. MPEG-4 is designed to work well over many transmission methods and at a wide range of transmission speeds.

Here are just a few of the exciting things MPEG-4 will allow:

▶ **Bitrate and bandwidth scalability**
In MPEG-4, a high bitrate stream will be able to be scaled down to a lower bitrate, or part of the frequency range of a stream could be discarded so that the stream is still coherent for someone receiving it over a slow network connection.

▶ **Error robustness**
MPEG-4 will be capable of handling transmission errors in a way that conceals them as much as possible.

▶ **Playing N-1 audio objects**
Because audio objects are distinct, a listener might not choose to hear all of them. For example, it could be used in a karaoke-like application (leaving out a single voice or instrument).

▶ **Text to speech**
MPEG-4 will include support for synthesized speech from text with optional descriptive information, such as language and dialect, age, gender, and speech rate of the speaker.

▶ **Score driven audio**
MPEG-4 will define structured audio tools that will be able to create sound using descriptions in the Structured Audio Orchestra Language (SAOL) and the Structured Audio Score Language (SASL). Unlike MIDI, in which the instrument voices are stored in the playback device, an MPEG-4 structured audio stream actually contains the information the playback device needs to recreate the instrument exactly as specified by the creator. This allows compositions to contain information needed to produce musical instruments (guitar, piano, and so on), sound effects (footsteps), simulated natural sounds (flowing water), or other custom effects from only a description.

Initial MPEG-4 standards were published in October 1998 and modified in December 1999, with additional work under way. Some MPEG-4 tools are beginning to become available, although not all functionality (especially functionality related to synthesized audio) is possible with current tools.

MPEG-7

The MPEG-7 standard will define a way of attaching descriptive information to the actual multimedia content so it can be more easily managed and searched. It is intended to complement the earlier MPEG standards rather than replace them. MPEG-7 is sometimes called the Multimedia Content Description Interface. The standard is scheduled to be completed and published in July 2001.

Q93 If I make an investment in MP3 now, what happens when the next hot format comes out?

What will happen when some new digital audio takes over from MP3 as the digital audio favorite? Will you end up with a hard drive full of useless files to delete, or CD-Rs full of MP3 files that you throw into a box in your basement, along with your old vinyl records and eight-track cassettes?

You won't really miss out on anything down the line if you purchase MP3 files now, or if you spend some time converting music to MP3 format. MP3 is so widespread that it's a pretty sure bet there will be players that can handle it for some time down the road. Because MP3 is media independent, you won't get stuck when the popular storage media changes, because it will be possible to simply transfer the MP3 files from the old media, like a CD-R disc, to the new media, whatever that may be. Additionally, audio saved as MP3 can always be converted to whatever the latest format is, although the sound quality of this kind of file will only be as good as the original MP3.

The portable or home audio MP3 player you buy now probably won't last. Although some portable devices now being sold have the capability to be upgraded to play new formats, there will be limits to how far this will go. At some point, the hardware won't be upgradable to the latest system, and you'll probably want a newer one that is even smaller and more convenient (and probably won't need onboard storage).

Glossary

Glossary

AAC
Advanced audio coding. An audio encoding method developed as part of the MPEG-2 standard. It is used in a number of proprietary digital audio schemes. **See Question 91.**

AHRA
The Audio Home Recording Act of 1992 allows consumers to create copies of recordings for personal, non-commercial use. **See Question 23.**

ANALOG AUDIO
A continuously varying representation of sound waves. In most analog audio systems, a continuously varying voltage signal represents the sound wave.

ATRAC3
Adaptive transform acoustic coding 3. An audio encoding method developed by Sony and based on the format used by MiniDisc players. See Question 91.

a2b MUSIC
A proprietary, secure music distribution system developed by AT&T. It uses AAC for compression. **See Question 91.**

BANDWIDTH
The capacity of a network or communication channel to carry information. High-speed Internet access using DSL or a cable modem provides much more bandwidth than older 56k modems, because much more information can be sent and received in the same amount of time.

Bit

A binary digit. Computers use the binary digits 0 and 1 to represent information internally. The more bits used to describe something, like an audio recording, the more storage space is needed to hold the sequence of bits that represent that thing.

Bitrate

The number of bits per a given time interval, used as a measure of information flow. Digital audio bitrate is often given in units of kbps (thousands of bits per second). **See Question 7.**

Buffer

A temporary storage space used as a reserve to insure a smooth flow of data. **See Question 78.**

Buffer underrun

The term used to describe a buffer running empty unintentionally. If a buffer underrun occurs when creating a CD-R, a "coaster" may be the result. If a buffer underrun occurs in a streaming MP3 player, there may be gaps or pauses in the music. **See Question 78.**

Burn

The process of writing to a CD-R is called "burning" the disc. **See Question 77.**

Byte

A unit of storage equal to 8 bits.

Cable modem

A high-speed modem that connects to an Internet service provider through cable TV lines instead of the telephone system. **See Question 29.**

CBR

Constant bitrate. A type of encoding that allocates the same number of bits per second of audio throughout the entire track. **See Question 73.**

CDDB

Compact disc database. A free online service which can be used by look up and retrieve album and track information for a particular compact disc. **See Question 76.**

CD-R

Compact disc-recordable. A type of compact disc which can be written to ("burned") once using a CD-R drive. **See Question 77.**

CD-RW

Compact disc-rewritable. A type of compact disc similar to a CD-R disc, but can be erased and re-used using a CD-RW drive. **See Question 78.**

Coaster

Slang for a junk CD-R disc from a failed write attempt. **See Question 79.**

Codec

A method implemented in software or hardware for encoding and decoding digital data.

CompactFlash

A type of memory card used by many portable consumer electronic devices including digital cameras and some MP3 players. **See Question 63.**

Compression

Representing data in a more efficient format so it takes up less space when stored and/or requires less bandwidth when transmitted. **See Question 7.**

DAM CD

A type of CD sold by MP3.com that includes audio tracks that can be played on a regular CD player as well as the same tracks in MP3 format. **See Question 32.**

Decoding

The process of converting a compressed audio format, like MP3, back into a form that can be played back. **See Question 10.**

Digital audio

Audio that has been sampled to get a number of data points that approximate the original analog sound waves. Digital audio must be converted back to analog form for playback.

Digital audio extraction (DAE)
Reading digital audio directly from a CD, as opposed to playing it back and sampling the analog signal. DAE is also called "ripping." **See Question 68.**

Digital rights management (DRM)
A system that can track and manage licensing and ownership of digital content. **See Question 89.**

Digital watermark
Bits spread throughout a digital file that can be used to include rights management information. **See Question 89.**

DMCA
Digital Millennium Copyright Act. Legislation that modified copyright law to make provisions for digital audio, including Webcasting. **See Question 25.**

DSL
Digital subscriber line. A type of high-speed data networking that can be run over regular telephone lines. **See Question 29.**

Encoding
The process of transforming audio into a compressed format, such as MP3. **See Question 9.**

Encryption
Coding data so it can only be read by someone with the correct decryption key. Encryption is often used in secure digital audio systems to prevent unauthorized distribution of files.

EPAC
Enhanced Perceptual Audio Coder. An audio encoding method developed by Lucent Technologies. **See Question 91.**

Fair use doctrine (of copyright law)
Provisions in copyright law for legal copying of content in certain situations without first gaining permission from the copyright owner. **See Question 22.**

Fraunhofer Institute for Integrated Circuits
A research lab that has been instrumental in developing audio coding methods including MP3 and AAC. **See Question 4.**

Freeware
A method of software distribution where the program is given away for no charge by the author.

FTP
File transfer protocol. A method of sending and receiving files from the Internet.

GB
Gigabyte. A unit of storage equal to 1,073,741,824 bytes.

ID3 Tag
A means of saving limited descriptive information, including title, performer, album name, year of release, and genre, along with an MP3 track. **See Question 75.**

ISO
International Organization for Standardization. An international body that works with national standards groups to create define common standards. **See Question 3.**

ISP
Internet service provider. A company that provides users with access to the Internet, usually for a monthly fee.

Jitter
Errors in synchronization in extracting digital audio from a CD that result in extraneous pops and clicks in the audio file. **See Question 71.**

Kb or KB
Kilobyte. A unit of storage equal to 1,024 bytes. However, see kbps.

kbps
Transfer rate of 1,000 bits per second. Here lowercase "k" indicates 1,000, rather than 1,024 as in "Kb."

KB/sec
Transfer rate of 1,024 bytes per second. See kbps.

http://www.muskalipman.com

Layer III
The most advanced of three closely related compression schemes defined by the audio portion of MPEG-1 and MPEG-2. MP3 is the common name used to describe audio that uses the Layer III compression. **See Question 4.**

List site
A Web site that provides links to many other sites with MP3 files, but doesn't provide any MP3 files itself. List sites are often used to link to pirated MP3 collections. **See Question 33.**

Liquid Audio
A widely used but proprietary digital audio system that uses MPEG-2 AAC. **See Question 91.**

Lossy compression
A type of data compression that does not keep all information is said to be "lossy." Many popular digital audio formats, including MP3, use lossy compression.

Masking
A psychoacoustic principle that certain portions of audio are inaudible because they are covered up, or "masked" by other parts of the audio. MP3 calculates the masked portions of audio so that they can be removed in order to compress the file. **See Question 8.**

MB
Megabyte. A unit of storage equal to 1,048,576 bytes.

Meta-search engine
A Web service that sends a single query to multiple search engines and provides a combined listing of all the results. **See Question 37.**

MP3
Commonly used name for the Motion Picture Experts Group Audio Layer III digital audio format.

MPEG
Motion Pictures Experts Group. A group of people who as part of ISO set standards for audio and video storage and transmission. **See Question 3.**

MPEG-1
An international standard for storage and retrieval of video and audio. **See Question 3.**

MPEG-2
An international standard for digital television. **See Question 3.**

MPEG-4
An international standard for multimedia applications. **See Question 92.**

MPEG-7
An international standard for describing multimedia information to aid in managing and searching that multimedia content. **See Question 92.**

MUSICAL WORK
Legal term for the written score and lyrics that make up a composition. **See Question 21.**

NET ACT
Amended copyright law to specify penalties for illegal copying and distributing of copyrighted by electronic means. **See Question 20.**

NET RADIO
A streaming audio broadcast on the Internet that is analogous to an over-the-air radio station. **See Question 55.**

NORMALIZATION
The process of adjusting the volume level on tracks as they are encoded, so that their peak levels fall within a similar range. **See Question 74.**

PARALLEL PORT
An interface for connecting external devices to an IBM-compatible computer. Some MP3 players use parallel port interfaces to download music. **See Question 78.**

PCM
Pulse Code Modulation. An uncompressed encoding method for digital audio. **See Question 1.**

Pirated Music
Music that is illegally copied or distributed without permission of the copyright owners.

Playlist
A listing of songs queued up to be played. A playlist can also be saved for reuse. **See Question 52.**

Plug-in
A software module that can be used to add additional functionality to an existing program. The Winamp player uses plug-ins to add special audio or visual effects. **See Question 47.**

Portal
A Web site that provides a good starting point for information and services, often specialized to cover a certain topic. **See Question 32.**

Psychoacoustics
The science of figuring out how we perceive sound. The MP3 coding scheme uses a psychoacoustic model when it determines which parts of the audio it can leave out of an MP3 encoded file. **See Question 8.**

Ratio Site
A download site that enforces an upload/download ratio. A person who wants to download a file from a ratio site must first upload one or more files. **See Question 34.**

RealAudio
A popular streaming format for audio and video developed by RealNetworks. **See Question 91.**

RIAA
Recording Industry Association of America. A trade organization that represents recording industry interests. **See Question 16.**

Ripping
Slang for digital audio extraction. **See Question 66.**

Sampling
The process of repeatedly measuring and storing a digital representation of an analog signal. **See Question 22.**

SDMI
Secure Digital Music Initiative. **See Question 90.**

Search engine
A Web service that allows users to query an index for links to Web sites that match their query. The index may cover a particular set of Web pages, or a large portion of the Web. **See Question 34.**

Shareware
A way of distributing software on the honor system. Shareware can be freely copied and downloaded, but users are usually expected to pay a small registration fee to the creator if they continue to use the software after a trial period.

SHOUTcast
A system for streaming MP3 audio that was developed by Nullsoft (now part of AOL). **See Question 57.**

Skin
A custom interface that can be added to software that changes the appearance, but not the functionality of the program. **See Question 47.**

SmartMedia
A type of small memory card used by many portable MP3 players for storage. **See Question 63.**

Sound recording
Legal term for a particular recording made of a song by a performer. The copyright for a sound recording is often owned by a record company. **See Question 21.**

Space-shifting
Moving or copying content between different media, formats, or devices. **See Question 23.**

Statutory license
A license that is granted by law rather than by the owner. **See Question 25.**

Streaming audio
Audio that is broadcast in a single, continuous feed. Streaming audio can be used to create a net radio station. **See Question 55.**

http://www.muskalipman.com

USB
Universal serial bus. An external interface that can be used to connect devices, like portable MP3 players, to a personal computer. **See Question 78.**

VBR
Variable bitrate. A type of encoding that adjusts the number of bits used to represent each second of audio according to the complexity of that portion of the music. **See Question 73.**

VQF
Transform-domain weighted interleave vector quanitization (TwinVQ). A digital audio format created by NTT. **See Question 91.**

WAV
An uncompressed sound file format for PCs. **See Question 1.**

WEBCASTING
Using the Internet to broadcast audio or multimedia content. **See Question 55.**

WINDOWS MEDIA AUDIO
A secure audio format developed by Microsoft that can be used for downloadable or streaming audio. **See Question 91.**

Index

Note: Italicized page numbers refer to illustrations, tables, figures, tips, or notes boxes. A glossary precedes this index.

2Wire (Web site) 57

A

a2b (audio format) 200–201
About.com Backup and Recovery (Web site) 97
accessing MP3s. *See* finding MP3s
Adaptive Transform Acoustic Coding 3 (ATRAC3) (audio format) 200
ADCs (analog-to-digital converters) 17
Advanced Audio Coding (AAC) (audio format) 200
AHRA (Audio Home Recording Act) of 1992 31
amp decoder 28, 29
analog audio
    converting to digital 17–19
    explanation of 16
analog audio extraction
    versus digital extraction 146, 159–160
    process of 151–153
analog-to-digital converters (ADCs) *17, 152*
AOL (America Online), merger with Time Warner 193
AOL's Spinner.com (Net radio portal) 128
appearance of MP3 players. *See* skins
ARTISTdirect network (portal site) 72
artists, recording
    effect of MP3 on 33–35
    effect of piracy on 46
    getting noticed by recording industry 187–188
    Net radio usage 186
    online promotion of 183–184
    resources for 186
    selection of well-known 90
    setting up Web site 56, 184–186
ASPI CD access method *159, 160*
ATRAC3 (Adaptive Transform Acoustic Coding 3) (audio format) 200
audio
    converting to MP3 format 151–153
    explanation of 16
    human perception of 19–21
AudioActive Production Studio (encoder) *149*
AudioCatalyst (ripper/encoder) *149*
    features of 146–147
    intermediate WAV option 162
    jitter correction in *160*
    normalization selection 164
    ripping and encoding integration 145
    using 155–156
AudioFind (MP3 search engine) 78
AudioGrabber (ripper/encoder) *164*
Audio Home Recording Act (AHRA) of 1992 31, 43
Audio Layer III (audio compression method) 12–13
AudioReQuest (home stereo) *177, 178*
auditory masking 19–21
automobiles, listening to MP3s in 136–137, 194

B

background noise
    and sampling resolution 18-19
    when capturing audio 153
backing up 97
bad links 80-81
bands, music. *See* artists, recording
bandwidth
    future increase of 193
    scalability of in MPEG-4 standard 203
BitLaw (Web site) 40
bitrate
    definition of 19
    in MPEG-4 standard 203
    and streaming audio 124-125
    suggested 162-163
    supported by MP3 22
    for various compression ratios 24
booking events 52
broadcasters, Net radio. *See* Net radio stations
browsing for MP3s 50, 51, 64. *See also* finding MP3s; searching for MP3s
Buchinger, Mark *107*
buffering 124
buffer size, of CD-R drives 171
buffer underruns *171*
burning CDs
    disc closing options 175
    explanation of expression *167*
    MP3 to WAV conversion 172-174
    process of 176
    testing 176
    write speed 175
buying MP3s
    advantages of 88-89
    disadvantages of 89-90
    process of 90-95
    receipts for 96
    Web sites for 85-88

C

cable modems 56, *57*
Cable-Modems.Org (Web site) *57*
cables
    computer to portable player 133-134
    computer to stereo 177
cars, listening to MP3s in 136-137, 194
cassette tapes, converting to MP3 format 151-153
CBR (Constant Bitrate Encoding) 162
CDDB (online CD database) 166
CDNOW (music retailer) 36
CD players, portable 132
CDPoint (online music store) 129
CD-R (CDRecordable) drive
    versus CD-RW (CD-ReWritable) 168-169
    important features 168-171
    purpose of 167
CD-ROMs
    buying MP3s on 59, 86-87
    digital audio extraction support 150
CD-RW (CD-ReWritable) drive 168-169
CDs (compact discs)
    converting to MP3 format. *See* ripping
    creating custom 87
    creating from MP3s. *See* burning CDs
    MP3 players utilizing 136
    online database of 166
    sound quality versus MP3s 25
Change Music Network (portal site) 66
channels, reducing number of 19
chat, online *64*, 82
clicks, in audio samples *160*
clips, sample 82-83
Close Disc option 175

Close Session and Leave Disc
  Open option 175
CNET (Web site) 102
code, source 28
CompactFlash cards 135
compression, sound
    advances in technology 26
    definition of 19
    process of 16-19
    and sound perception 19-21
    versus sound quality 23-24
    and stereo modes 22
computing, pervasive 194
connection, Internet
    and download speed 55-57
    and streaming audio 124-125
Constant Bitrate Encoding (CBR) 162, 163
Consumer Electronics Show
  (trade show) 192
consumers
    benefits of MP3 for 36
    rights of 32
converting
    audio from non-CD sources 151-153
    CDs to MP3. *See* ripping
    MP3s to WAV 172-174
copying music. *See* downloading MP3s;
  ripping
copy protection scheme 43
copyright law 38-39, 41
    See also law suits
    and "fair use" 42
    for streaming MP3s 44-45, 181
cost considerations 88
crashes, computer 97-98
Creative Labs NOMAS
  (portable MP3 player) 139
Creative Labs Soundblaster Live
  (sound card) 102
criticism, music 42

cybertropix (meta-search site) 81
Cynic Project, The (Web site) *35*

D

DAE. *See* digital audio extraction
DAM CDs 59, 86-87
data backup 97
database, online CD 166
data compression. *See* compression,
  sound
Dave Matthews Band (recording group) *40*
decoder source code. *See* source code
decoding process 14, *15, 23*
default player, setting *113*
descriptive information, MP3 165, 166
Diamond Multimedia (company)
  31, *43, 44*
Diamond Multimedia Rio 500
  (portable MP3 player) 138
Diamond Multimedia Rio PMP 300
  (portable MP3 player) 138
digital audio, converting analog
  audio to 17
digital audio extraction (DAE)
    See also ripping
    versus analog extraction 159-160
digital audio formats
    future of 195-196
    non-MP3 199-204
Digital Millennium Copyright Act (DMCA)
  of 1998 45, 122-123
digital signal processing (DSP) plug-ins *107*
digital watermarks 195, *196*
Disc-at-Once option 175
DiscJockey.com (Net radio portal) 129
distributing own music. *See* promotion
  of recording artists

http://www.muskalipman.com

DMCA (Digital Millennium Copyright Act) of 1998 45
Download Demon (download utility) *60*
downloading MP3s
    See also finding MP3s
    illegally 30-32, 40, 46
        and claims of legality *75*
        sites for 53
    and Internet speed 55-57
    legally 37-40, 43
    re-downloading 97-98
    scheduling 60-61
DOWNLOADSdirect (Web site) 72
drive speed, of CD-R drives 169
DSL connections 56, *57*
DSP (digital signal processing) plug-ins *107*

E

Eclectic CP-200 (portable MP3 player) 140
educational campaign, on legal use of MP3 38
educational use of music 42
electrical signals, analog 16-17
EMI Music (recording company) 33
empeg player (MP3 player) 136-137
EMusic.com (portal site)
    buying MP3s on
        general explanation 85-86
        step-by-step process 90-95
    e-mail receipt from 96
    features of 68
encoding
    Constant Bitrate Encoding (CBR) 162, 163
    definition of 144
    process of 22-23
    ripping to WAV file before 161-162
    setting track information 165
    software for 146-149
        settings and options 156-159
        using 155-156
    suggested method 162-163
    Variable Bitrate Encoding (VBR) 163
Enhanced Perceptual Audio Coder (EPAC) (audio format) 33, 201
events, promoting and booking 52
expense considerations 88
extensions, file 80

F

"fair use" 42
Farmclub.com (Web site) 188
file associations *113*
file extensions, MP3 80
finding MP3s
    See also searching for MP3s
    according to personal taste 82-83
    by "influence" 70
    methods for 50-51
    on MP3-related sites 51-54
    software for 83-84
Fisher (music band) 35
formats, digital audio
    future of 195-196
    non-MP3 199-204
Frankel, Justin 28
Fraunhofer Institute for Integrated Circuits (Germany) 13, 25, 26, 28
FreeAmp (MP3 player) *29*
Free MP3 Files (MP3 list site) 76
free source code 28, *29*
freeware software *103*
frequency, sampling 17-18
FTP clients *77*

future of digital audio
    digital audio devices 191-193
    digital audio formats 195-196
    increased bandwidth 193
    music distribution 197
    pervasive computing 194

G

Gadget Labs (computer peripheral provider) 102
GeoCities (Web hosting service) 186
Grateful Dead, The (music band) *40*
Greely, Dave 179
groups, music. *See* artists, recording

H

hard disks, on portable MP3 players 136
hardware requirements 101-102
Harry Fox Agency (copyright licensing company) 41
Headlight Software GetRight (download utility) *60*
headphones 102
history of MP3 28-30
Hitsquad.com Shareware Music Machine (Web site) 153
HomeRecording.com (Web site) 153, 187
hosting services, Web site 186
Huffman coding 22
hyperlinks to MP3 sites
    See also list sites, MP3
    bad links 80-81

I

iCASTER media player 127
iCAST (online media company) 29, 127

Icecast (software) *29*
ID3 tags 89, 165, 166
IDE/EIDE/ATAPI interface, for CD-R drives 170
illegal copying of music 30-32, 40, 46
    and claims of legality *75*
    sites for 53
iMusic (Web site) 72
independent artists
    effect of MP3 on 34-35
    on MP3.com 64-65
International Organization for Standardization (ISO) 10-12
Internet connection
    and download speed 55-57
    future of 193
    and streaming audio 124-125
Internet server 56
Internet Underground Music Archive (IUMA) 69, 184
ISDN connections 56
ISO (International Organization for Standardization) 10-12
IUMA (Internet Underground Music Archive) 69, 184

J

Jimmy and Doug's Farmclub.com (Web site) 188
jitter, in audio samples *160*
joint stereo mode *22*

K

Kemp, Eric 165
Kemp, Kurt Andrew *40*
Kerbango Internet Radio 178, 192, *193*
Kohn on Music Licensing (book) 40

L

law suits
    See also copyright law
    against MP3 archive sites 30–32
    RealNetworks vs. Streambox 125
    RIAA vs. Diamond Multimedia 31, 43, *44*
    RIAA vs. Napster.com 84
Leave Session Open option 175
legal use of MP3 37–40
    converting from CD to MP3 44
    copying onto more than one computer/device 43
    streaming by Net radio stations 44–45
Library of Congress Copyright Office (Web site) 45
licensing. *See* copyright law; legal use of MP3
Lindahl, Andreas *107*
links to MP3 sites
    See also list sites, MP3
    bad links 80–81
Liquid Audio (audio format) 201
Listen.com (digital music directory) 33, 74, 88
listening to MP3s. *See* MP3 players; Net radio stations
list sites, MP3 53
    examples of 75–76
    problems with 75
Live365.com (streaming audio service) 126–127, *181*
LP records, converting to MP3 format 151–153
Lycos MP3 Search (MP3 search engine) 54, 78

M

MacAMP (MP3 player). *See* MACAST
MACAST (MP3 player)
    comparison with other players *105*
    features of 111
Macintosh computers, MP3 players for *105*
    MP3 players for 111
masking, auditory 19–21
memory cards, for portable MP3 players 134–136
message boards *64*, 82
meta-search sites 81
microdrives 136
microphones *151*
Microsoft's Windows Media (audio format) 124
Mjuice (Web site) 88
modems 56, 58
movement, MP3. *See* popularity of MP3
MP3
    general explanation of 8–9
    meaning of abbreviation 10, 12–13
MP3 Anyware (computer/stereo peripheral) 177
MP3Board.com (MP3 search site) 78
MP3 Car (Web site) *137*
MP3.com (portal site) 51–52, 64–65
    buying MP3s on 86–87
    creating own Web site within 184–185
    DAM CDs on 59
MP3 Corner, The (MP3 list Web site) *53*
MP3now (portal site) 67, *79*
MP3 players
    See also portable MP3 players
    and file associations *113*
    hardware requirements 101–102
    most popular *105*
    playing MP3 files 112–114

setting as default player *113*
setting track information 165
skins for *104*, 107
volume control 115
for Windows 106-110
MP3 Resource, The (MP3 list site) 76
MPEG-3 standard 13
MPEG-4 standard 203-204
MPEG-7 standard 203
MPEG (Motion Picture Experts Group) 10-12
- Audio Web site 200
- incorporating technological advances 26
- new standards 202-204

MSCDEX CD access method *159, 160*
Multimedia Content Description Interface 204
MusicDish (Web site) 187
musicians. See artists, recording
Musicland (music to music retailer) 33
MusicMaker (Web site) 87
MusicMatch Jukebox (MP3 player/ripper/encoder)
- comparison with other players *105*
- features of 109
- file associations *113*
- jitter correction in *160*
- ripping and encoding features 145, 147-149
- settings and options 157-158
- use with portable players *133*

music servers 176-178
Mutschler, Michael 165

N

Napster (software) 83-84
NET (No Electronic Theft) Act 40

NetRadio.com (Net radio station) 129
Net radio stations
- *See also* streaming audio
- audio formats for 123-124
- creating own 179-181
- explanation of 121-122
- finding 126-129
- laws for streaming MP3s by 44-45, 181
- popularity of 122-123
- promoting artists with 186

Netzip Download Demon (download utility) *60*
news reporting, and copyright law 42
No Electronic Theft (NET) Act 40
noise, background
- producing 19-20
- and sampling resolution 18-19
- when capturing audio 153

Noise-to-Mask Ratio (sound quality measurement) 25
nolo.com (Web site) 40
NOMAD (portable MP3 player) *133*, 139
normalization 164
Notes box 3
Nullsoft SHOUTcast (MP3 server) 123, 179
Nullsoft's SHOUTcast (MP3 server) 123
Nullsoft WaveOut plug-in *119*
Nyquist Theorem 17-18

O

Online Broadcasting Power! (book) 179
online ticketing 52
opening MP3 files 112-114
open source code 28, *29*
Output plug-in selection, in Winamp *119*

http://www.muskalipman.com

P

Palavista (meta-search site) 81
parallel ports 133, 170
Patterson Designs (software provider) 58
pay-per-listen systems 197
PCM (Pulse Code Modulation) 8-9
performance licenses 188
pervasive computing 194
Phish (music band) *40*
pictures, in MP3 files 89
pirating of music 30-32, 40, 46
players, MP3. *See* MP3 players
playing MP3 files 112-114
playlists 109, 116-117
Play-Media Systems (software developer) 29
plug-ins *104*
    for MusicMatch Jukebox 109
    table of MP3 players compatible with *105*
    using 118-119
    for Winamp 107
popularity of MP3
    reasons for 14-15, 28-30
    recording industry's reaction to 30-33
portable CD players 132
portable MP3 players 131
    average cost 132
    best available 138-140
    memory of 134-136
    versus portable CD players 132
    transferring music from computer to 133-134
portal sites 51, 64-65. *See also names of specific portal sites*
processor speed, computer 101
Production Studio (encoder) *149*
programming instructions. *See* source code
promotion of recording artists 183-184
    getting noticed by recording industry 187-188
    with Net radio 186
    resources for 187
    setting up Web site 184-186
psychoacoustics, and sound compression 19-21
Pulse Code Modulation (PCM) 8-9
purchasing MP3s. *See* buying MP3s

Q

quality, sound
    determining 24-25
    MP3s versus CDs 25
    sound compression versus 23-24

R

radio stations, Net. *See* Net radio stations
Raitio, Samuel *107*
ratio sites *77*
RealAudio (audio format) 124, 201
RealJukebox (MP3 player)
    comparison with other players *105*
    features of 110
    file associations *113*
RealJukebox (MP3 player/ripper/encoder) *149*
RealNetworks' Basic Server G2 *180*
RealNetworks' RealAudio (audio format) 124, 201
recording industry
    effect of MP3 on 30-33, 46
    electronic distribution of music by 33
    getting noticed by 187-188
Recording Industry Association of America (RIAA) 30-32, 45, 181
records, LP 151-153

record stores, effect of MP3 on 35–36
reporting, and copyright law 42
resolution, sampling 18–19
Resources for Tape Traders (Web site) *40*
retail record stores, effect of MP3 on 35–36
reviews, music
    and copyright law 42
    Web sites with *64*
RIAA (Recording Industry Association of America) 30–32, 45, 181
Riffage.com (Web site) 185
Rio 500 (portable MP3 player) 138
Rio PMP 300 (portable MP3 player) 138
Rio (portable MP3 player) 31, 43, *44*
RioPort (Web site) 73
ripping
    CD-ROM support for 150
    definition of 144
    legally 44
    software for 146–149
        settings and options 156–159
        using 155–156
    troubleshooting problems with 150
    to WAV file 161–162
RollingStone.com (portal site) 70, *71*, 185
rome (MP3 player) 137

S

SamGoody.com (music retailer) 33
sample clips 82–83
sampling
    and copyright law 42
    explanation of process 17
    frequency of 17–18
    resolution of 18–19
SAOL (Structured Audio Orchestra Language) 204
SASL (Structured Audio Score Language) 204

saving, streaming audio 125
Sawyer, Ben 179
scheduling downloads 60–61
SCMS (serial copy management system) 31
SCSI interface, for CD-R drives 170
SDMI (Secure Digital Music Initiative)
    future of 196, 198–199
    history of 31, 32, 197
searching for MP3s 50, 51, 54.
See also finding MP3s
    bad links and 80–81
    by "influence" 70
    on multiple sites simultaneously 81
    search engine Web sites 77–78
    software for 83–84
    tips for 79–80
    Web sites with capabilities for *64*
Secure Digital Music Initiative (SDMI).
See SDMI (Secure Digital Music Initiative)
SeekMP3.com (meta-search site) 81
seeUthere.com (event-planning Web site) 52
serial copy management system (SCMS) 31
server, Internet 56
shareware software *103*
SHOUTcast (MP3 server) 123, 179
SHOUTcast Showcase (Net radio directory) 126–127
simple stereo mode 22
singers. *See* artists, recording
sites, Web. *See* Web sites
skins, for MP3 players *104*
    MP3 players compatible with *105*
    for Sonique 108
    using 117
    for Winamp 107
SmartMedia cards 134–135
Software GetRight (download utility) *60*
software, shareware and freeware *103*
solid state floppy disk cards (SSFDC) 134–135

http://www.muskalipman.com

songwriters. *See* artists, recording
Sonique (MP3 player)
    comparison with other players *105*
    features of 108
    file associations *113*
Sony's Adaptive Transform Acoustic Coding 3 (ATRAC3) (audio format) 200
sound
    See also audio; compression, sound; quality, sound
    explanation of 16
    human perception of 19–21
Soundblaster Live (sound card) 102, 152
SoundByting campaign 38
sound cards 102, *151*, 152
SoundJam MP (MP3 player/ripper/encoder) *105*, 111, 149
source code 28, *29*
space-shifting of music 43
speakers, computer 102
speed of downloads 55–57
Spinner.com (Net radio portal) 128
SSFDC (solid state floppy disk cards) 134–135
statutory license 45
stereo modes 22
stereo system
    of future 176
    turning into music server 176–178
    volume control 115
stores, record 35–36
StreamboxVCR (software) 125
streaming audio
    See also Net radio stations
    disadvantages of 124–125
    explanation of 59, 121–122
    formats for 123–124
    and Internet connection 124–125
    laws for 44–45, 181
    saving 125

StreamWorks (MP3 server) 179
Structured Audio Orchestra Language (SAOL) 204
Structured Audio Score Language (SASL) 204
suits, law. *See* law suits
Suncoast.com (music retailer) 33
Supertracks (company) 33

T

tape, cassette 151–153
text, in MP3 files 89
themes, for MP3 players. *See* skins
Thompson Multimedia (company) 26
ticketing, online 52
Time Warner (media company), merger with AOL 193
Tips box 3
Top 25 MP3 Sites (MP3 list site) 76
track information 165, 166
trading, music *40*
Transform-domain Weighted Interleave Vector Quantization (TwinVQ) (audio format) 202
Tripod (Web hosting service) 186
TurboMP3 (portable MP3 player) 140
Turtle Beach (software/hardware provider) 102
tutorials, MP3 *64*
TweakDUN (software) 58
TwinVQ (Transform-domain Weighted Interleave Vector Quantization) (audio format) 202

U

Ultimate Band List (UBL) (Web site) 72
United States Copyright Office 39

Universal Music Group
(recording company) 33
Universal Music Group
(recording compete) 73
Universal Serial Bus (USB) 170
uploading MP3s *77*
USB (Universal Serial Bus) 134, 170
U.S. Copyright Office 39
Uzelac, Tomislav *29*

V

Variable Bitrate Encoding (VBR) 163
vehicles, listening to MP3s in 136–137, 194
Vertical Horizon Eclectic CP-200
(portable MP3 player) 140
Virgin Megastores (music retailer) 36
volume control 115, 164
Voquette Media Manager (software) 125
Vormbrock, Alex *107*
VQF (Transform-domain Weighted Interleave Vector Quantization) (audio format) 202

W

watermarks, digital 195, *196*
Wave Balance control 115
WAV files 8–9
    converting MP3s to 172–174
    ripping to 161–162
Webcasting. *See* Net radio stations
Web Licensing FAQ, of RIAA 45
Webnoize (Web site) 187
Web sites
    See also list sites; *names of specific Web sites;* portal sites
    for buying MP3s 85–88
    hosting services 186

    meta-search 81
    MP3-related 51–54
    putting MP3 files on 41
    ratio sites *77*
    for recording artists, setting up 184–186
    search engine 77–78
Winamp (MP3 player)
    comparison with other players *105*
    features of 106–107
    file associations *113*
    history of 28
    opening MP3 files 112–114
    playlists 116–117
    using plug-ins with 118–119
    volume control 115
Windows Media (audio format) 124
Windows Media Audio (WMA) 202
Windows, MP3 players for *105*, 106–110

X

Xing AudioCatalyst (ripper/encoder).
    See AudioCatalyst (ripper/encoder)
Xing StreamWorks (MP3 server) 179

Y

Yahoo! broadcast (Net radio portal) 128
Yesterday USA (Net radio portal) 129

Z

ZD Net (Web site) 102
ZLook4 (MP3 search site) 78

http://www.muskalipman.com

MUSKA & LIPMAN

Order our free catalog by visiting
http://www.muskalipman.com

Order Form

Postal Orders:
Muska & Lipman Publishing
P.O. Box 8225
Cincinnati, Ohio 45208

On-Line Orders or more information:
http://www.muskalipman.com
Fax Orders:
(513) 924-9333

Qty.	Title	ISBN	Price	Total Cost
_____	*ICQ FYI*	1-929685-04-1	$14.95	_____
_____	*Cakewalk Power!*	1-929685-02-5	$29.95	_____
_____	*MP3 Power! with Winamp*	0-9662889-3-9	$29.99	_____
_____	*Digital Camera Solutions*	0-9662889-6-3	$29.95	_____
_____	*Scanner Solutions*	0-9662889-7-1	$29.95	_____

Subtotal _____

Sales Tax _____
(please add 6% for books shipped to Ohio addresses)

Shipping _____
($5.00 for US and Canada, $10.00 other countries)

TOTAL PAYMENT ENCLOSED _____

Ship to:
Company _____

Name _____

Address _____

City _____

State _____ Zip _____ Country _____

E-mail _____

Educational facilities, companies, and organizations interested in multiple copies of these books should contact the publisher for quantity discount information. Training manuals, CD-ROMs, electronic versions, and portions of these books are also available individually or can be tailored for specific needs.

Thank you for your order.